WISE WORDS
Insightful Reflections

Deborah Morrison & Arvind Singh

Manor House

Wise Words

Library and Archives Canada Cataloguing in Publication

Morrison, Deborah
 Wise words : insightful reflections / Deborah Morrison & Arvind Singh.

ISBN 978-1-897453-21-6

 1. Self-actualization (Psychology)--Quotations, maxims, etc. I. Singh, Arvind, 1970- II. Title.

BF637.S4M675 2012   158.1   C2012-907724-0

Published November 15, 2012: Manor House Publishing Inc., 452 Cottingham Crescent, Ancaster, ON, CANADA, L9G 3V6   905-648-2193 wwww.manor-house.biz

All rights reserved

Cover Design: Donovan Davie based on original art created and supplied by Kati Molin/Shutterstock

 We acknowledge the financial support of the Government of Canada through the Canada Book Fund (CBF) for our publishing activities.

Special thanks to the following contributors: Shri Rakesh Bhai, Robert-Anthony Browne, Donovan Davie: Michael B. Davie; James Deahl, Roeland Peter Hommerson, Ywaraj Singh Jina, Satish Kaku, Raj Kamal, Surjit Kaur, Tony Kent, Pastor Benjamin Wamalwa Khaemba, Hope Leon, Bob Lumbers, Vicky Mac Clean, Shelley Kay Manos, Angie Milki, Anthony Monaco, Wanda Morgan, Emily Mumma, Tracey Farrell Munro, Edane Padme, Michael Richards, Onkar Singh, Jennifer Vermeer, Ed Woods

Other Manor House titles by the same authors:
Mystical Poetry, **Deborah Morrison**
In The Garden: Where Inspiration Grows, **Deborah Morrison**
Nexus, **Deborah Morrison & Arvind Singh**
The Law of Attraction: Making it Work For You, **Morrison & Singh**
Web: www.holisticjourney2wealth.com / www.catchthespiritmediagroup.com

Wise Words

… Our intent is to bring

INSPIRATION

To billions of beings

Throughout the Universe

ENDORSEMENTS

"*WISE WORDS* is an eclectic, unique, and inspiring mix of quotes ranging from highly spiritual to everyday practical. *WISE WORDS* gives hope and offers hints at ways to change America and the world."
- Thom Hartmann, Progressive American Radio Host,
Author of *The Last Hours of Ancient Sunlight*
www.thomhartmann.com

"In these turbulent times of change and things coming apart, this collection of *WISE WORDS* extends a pool of warm thoughts from our elders that will comfort and sustain us as we create a new cultural mythos for the next cycle of ages that is almost upon us ..."
- Hank Wesselman, PhD
Anthropologist and Award-Winning Author of
Awakening to the Spirit World (with Sandra Ingerman);
The Spirit Walker Trilogy; and *The Bowl of Light*
www.hankwesselman.com

"While it is always edifying to be reminded of the words of writers such as Shakespeare, Goethe, Kahlil Gibran, and Joseph Campbell, the real gift of *WISE WORDS* is that it introduces its readers to the wisdom of many lesser known thinkers like Moribei Ueshiba, Uwaraj Singh Jina, and Sri Gordhan. Full marks go to the contributors as well as the editors. Deborah Morrison and Arvind Singh clearly understand the difference between quotes that, on first reading, merely sound profound, and those that are actually helpful to people who are living their lives in these confusing and conflicting times."
- James Deahl, Award- Winning Author of more than twenty literary titles including *Rooms the Wind Makes;*
North of Belleville; and *Opening the Stone Heart*

Foreword

By Michael B. Davie

Deborah Morrison and **Arvind Singh** have done it again!

The co-authors have created a new insightful and enlightening, inspiring book, fresh on the heels of their highly successful *The Law of Attraction – Making it Work for You!*

Their latest offering, *Wise Words,* offers the authors' own compelling thoughts, experiences and stories interwoven with the inspiring stories and thoughts of others, including truly enlightening quotations and expressions from some of the world's most influential and society-changing thinkers of all time.

All of this is of tremendous value to readers seeking to broaden their own appreciation and understanding of themselves and the world around them. *Wise Words* is more than mere food for thought – it's an absolute feast of knowledge, enlightenment and insightful reflections.

Of particular interest is the fact that *Wise Words* goes beyond the conventional and expected to share amazing wisdom from lesser known thinkers. As esteemed author James Deahl observes: "While it is always edifying to be reminded of the words of writers such as Shakespeare, Goethe, Kahlil Gibran, and Joseph Campbell, the real gift of *WISE WORDS* is that it introduces its readers to the wisdom of many lesser known thinkers like Moribei Ueshiba, Uwaraj Singh Jina, and Sri Gordhan. Full marks go to the contributors as well as the editors. Deborah Morrison and Arvind Singh clearly understand the difference between quotes that, on first reading, merely sound profound, and those that are actually helpful to people who are living their lives in these confusing and conflicting times."

Also of interest are the many seemingly ordinary people who contributed compelling stories and observations to this remarkable book.

The choice of quotations from the very famous and less-famous are all carefully and well selected.

It is true of this entire book that there is not a single page that will not have you, the reader, pondering its meaning and significance and applying its inherent wisdom to reflections on your own life.

This is a book filled with thoughtful and thought-provoking observations on the human condition and every aspect involved with it. Following its wisdom is to lead a fuller and more rewarding life.

It's a book for our times – and all times.

Wise Words is very highly recommended.

- **Michael B Davie**, author, *Winning Ways*

Introduction

Inspiration through Quotations

*"There are only two ways to live life.
One is as though nothing is a miracle.
The other is as though everything is a miracle"*
- Albert Einstein

A book can be long. Quotes are very short, and they capture the essence of a message in a condensed form. So having the right quote at the right time can change your perception or perspective, create expanded awareness, and transformation in your life.

Circumstances in your life may be joyous or sorrowful. You may be living in times of great joy, comfort and ease or you may find yourself experiencing extreme sorrow, challenges or suffering. To cope with varied life experience, along with quotes, you may discover infinite sources of inspiration. Return to these sources of inspiration in order to live through joyful times with wisdom. Find a way to connect with a source of inspiration when living through times of suffering. You will find that life's joys and challenges all become a part of your journey to wellness, so that you may experience Soul growth. Then with renewed insight and wisdom you will manifest increased joy and happiness in your life.

Amanda Goldston suggests a variety of ways to heighten your feeling of inspiration such as: to look at the wonders of nature, notice beauty, read poems, find quotes, listen to gentle/relaxing music, or enjoy beautiful artwork.

Michael Dooley shares an inspired perspective on life with the following quote: *"Never compromise a dream. Do what you must. The fears, beasts, and mountains before you are part of the plan. Stepping stones to a promised land. To a time and place that is so*

much closer than you expect. So don't let your eyes deceive you, for even as you read these words, your ship swiftly approaches..."
Michael Dooley

Inspiration overflows so that you will not only uplift yourself, but also assist others along their way through the inevitable "peaks" and "valleys" of life's journey. It is sometimes with the smallest fragment of inspiration that you are able to bring a ray of light into a situation. By doing so, you rekindle a feeling of hope and faith that enlightens the next steps for yourself or another, with ease, compassion, and peace.

Truly, the source of inspiration is infinite. In times of joy you may experience inspiration through healing, feeling younger, being more energized, or experiencing synchronicity and seeing that things are really working in your life and coming together with abundance. Also, through times of sorrow you may experience inspiration through meditation, prayer, discovering inner peace, or with wisdom from your Higher Self.

Always, a greater connection with your source of inspiration leads to a more complete giving and receiving of energies such as faith, hope, charity, and love. Through such inspiration there is healing, and then spontaneity of your own inner gifts & your true nature will have a chance to flow.

According to the Oxford Dictionary, "to inspire" means "to put uplifting thoughts, feelings or aims into something" or "to fill with creative power" or "to create a feeling or urge or ability to do something" or "to animate, encourage, arouse, stimulate, or motivate."

When inspired you awaken feelings of creativity, get ideas and act on them, experiences flow with ease, and opportunities show up. Joseph Campbell suggests that *"in times of difficulty, if you bring love to that experience and not discouragement, then you will find that strength is there. As you survive a disaster there is improvement in your stature, your character, and your life. Eventually, when you look back you will see that the moments that seemed to be the greatest failures were, in fact, what shaped the good in life you have now."*

In extreme situations you can sometimes feel like you are going through a disaster. Instead of *catastrophizing* an event, or what *may* happen in the future, try to gain some enhanced perspective:

"Nothing can happen to you that is not positive. Even though it looks and feels at the moment like a negative crisis, it is not."
Joseph Campbell

Quotes are exceptionally powerful, since, through the inspiring and healing power of the written word, you may awaken to dream as far as your heart can see. Know that whatever you dream you can do. Be guided by your Heart and Soul.

It is with passion and gratitude that we have compiled this collection of inspiring quotes and true life stories: so that you will find the inspiration to create more of what you want in your life, and begin to live more of your heart's desire. As you journey from day to day know that you have a gift that only you can give the world.

In our heart of hearts we want you to flourish...to be inspired...to embrace life, family, and friends more than ever before.

Our hope and wish is that Love will light your way with an abundance of bright blessings...

WISE WORDS is a fascinating collection of quotes and true life story contributions that will kindle a renewed sense of inspiration and hope in your life!

Be Inspired, - Deborah Morrison & Arvind Singh

Bibliography

Campbell, Joseph	*If You Bring Inspiration* (Article)
Goldston, Amanda	*What Is Inspiration, And What Inspires You* May 25th, 2008

Table of Contents
Further *Works by*..*4*
Deborah Morrison & Arvind Singh *4*
CREDITS..*4*
Many thanks to the following individuals for joining in the co-creative process of bringing **WISE WORDS** *from dream to reality* *4*
Introduction *6*
Inspiration through Quotations *6*
SPIRIT
Spirit - Chapter 1
Spiritual Quotes *14*
Authenticity 14
True Life Story by Tracey Farrell Munro................ 14
Freedom..15
True Life Story by Pastor Benjamin Wamalwa Khaemba 16
"What we do in life, echoes in eternity" 16
Fountain of God's Grace Revival Ministries is a non-profit Christian organization founded by God's servant Benjamin Wamalwa Khaemba, who is called by God to preach and teach the word of Hope, Grace, and Encouragement, bringing nations into spiritual practice, for children in all areas of life … in the spirit of Gladness and simplicity of Heart, by informing them to be Joyful in Hope, for in Hope we were saved. As a non-profit Christian organization, Fountain of God's Grace Revival Ministries' heart-beat is to bring Hope and Grace to the Hopeless in all areas of life..17
Grief / Sadness / Sorrow / Loss 17
Infinity / Timelessness... 18
Innocence / Child 20
Meditation / Awareness / Reflection......................23
Original Quote by Onkar Singh 23
Quotes on Meditation / Awareness / Reflection 24
Wise Words
10
Peace / Contentment / Silence / Equanimity / Inner Guidance
....25

True Life Story by Vicky Mac Lean 25
Quotes about Peace / Contentment / Silence / Equanimity / Inner Guidance..............................26
Purpose / Mission / Values / Ethics 30
True Life Story/Quote by Ed Woods 30
Quotes about Purpose / Mission / Values / Ethics / Goals 32
Self-worth / Self-esteem / Confidence 34
True Life Story by Jennifer Vermeer 34
Quotes on Self-worth / Self-esteem / Confidence.....35
Spontaneity / Opportunity / Flexibility ….. 37
Vision / Ideal..37
Wholeness / Oneness / Unity.................................38
True Life Story on Unity by Anthony Monaco 38
Quotes on Wholeness / Oneness / Unity 40
AIR
AIR – Chapter 2..44
Psychological Quotes..44
Attention / Focus / Present Moment 44
Belief 45
Character / Virtue / Dignity 46
Imagination / Dreaming 48
Positive Thinking / Optimism / Attitude 49
True Life Story by Angie Milki 49
True Life Story by James Deahl 50
Quotes on Positive Thinking / Optimism / Attitude 52
Thought / Mind 53

Wise Words
11

Wisdom / Insight / Knowledge / Discernment / Judgment 55
FIRE
FIRE – *Chapter 3*..57
FIRE...................................
True Life Story by Roeland Peter Hommerson 58
Emotional Quotes..61
Compassion / Kindness / Empathy / Sympathy / Charity 62
True Life Story by Yuwaraj Singh Jina....................62

Quotes on Compassion / Kindness / Empathy..........62
Sympathy / Charity..62
Co-Creation / Co-operation / Connectedness / Interdependence 66
Devotion / Sincerity 67
Emotions / Feelings...68
Forgiveness 69
Friendship 71
True Life Story by Emily Mumma..........................71
Quotes on Friendship..72
Asking / Giving / Receiving 74
Heart 75
Humility..76
Love
Marriage / Family / Stages of Development.................80
Non-Violence..83
Passion / Anger / Hate..83
Prayer 84
Purification 85
Relationships / Community 86
Wise Words
12
Responsibility 86
Service / Altruism / Healing 87
True Life Story by Bob Lumbers 88
Favourite Quote by Bill Vick..................................89
Quotes on Transformation / Personal Growth & Power 89
Trust / Faith..91
True Life Story by Wanda Morgan..........................91
Quotes on Trust / Faith...92
WATER
WATER – Chapter 4 ....
Acceptance / Harmony / Balance / Centeredness / Grounding / Moderation...94
Desire / Drives / Passions / Pleasures / Will.................99
Determination / Courage / Strength / Motivation / Willpower 101
Discipline / Self-Control / Mastery........................103
True Life Story by Raj Kamal 103
True Life Story by Michael Richards....................104

Quotes on Challenges / Adversity / Overcoming / Suffering / Pain..110
Encouragement / Hope...................................114
True Life Story by Hope S. Leon......................114
Quotes on Encouragement / Hope....................115
Flowing / Change / Impermanence / Emptiness / Temporality 117
True Life Story by Edane Padme 117
Quotes on Flowing / Change / Impermanence / Emptiness / Temporality...119
Leadership 121

EARTH
Earth – Chapter 5 ....*122*
Nature / Environment / Animals 123
Life / Experience / Living................................125
Wealth / Finances / Money / Material Possessions / Abundance 129
True Life Story by Surjit Kaur..........................129
Quotes on Wealth / Finances / Money / Material Possessions / Abundance 129
Gratitude / Blessing / Gifts / Grace / Destiny............137
Health 145
Humour / Laughter...146
Patience...148
Simplicity..148
Social Justice / Social Issues...........................150
Success / Accomplishment / Achievement / Excellence 153
True Life Story by Surjit Kaur..........................153
"Excellence is doing ordinary things extraordinarily well."
—John W. Gardner *153*
True Life Story by Robert-Anthony Browne..........153
Quotes on Success / Accomplishment / Achievement / Excellence...158
Sustainability 160
True Life Story on Action by Raj Kamal 161
True Life Story by Shelley Kay Manos................162
Quotes on Action / Ability / Work / Duty / Career / Vocation 162

A teacher who is indeed wise does not bid you to enter the house of his wisdom but rather leads you to the threshold of your mind.
~ Kahil Gibran

He is richest who is content with the least, for content is the wealth of nature.
~ Socrates

SPIRIT

Spiritual Quotes – Chapter One

The qualities in this chapter are touched by Spirit, where you get in touch with the core of who you are and learn to live from there. You intone: "I Am" based on your experience of self-awareness, self-consciousness. As you read the quotes in this chapter, get in touch with *Spiritual* qualities under the various topics and true life stories contained in this chapter.

The Spirit domain asks that we start with Inner Peace; reconnect with joy, innocence and silence within your Being. Ken Wilber captures the principle of the Spiritual journey in the following quote:

- Spirit slumbers in nature, awakens in mind, and finally recognizes itself as Spirit in the transpersonal domains *(Ken Wilber, A Brief History of Everything, 1996).*

Authenticity

True Life Story by Tracey Farrell Munro
To Thine own self be true   - **Shakespeare**

My mother would say this to us regularly – yet it was something she could not do. Because most mothers want what is best and better for their children, it was most likely the motherly nurturing aspect of her that was speaking – although she was not a very motherly or nurturing mother. I, the youngest of four and most precarious, intuitive and artistic child, witnessed a continual build up of her own self-created masks along with varied addictive behaviours accompanying those masks. I continuously tried to be close to her so I would say or do things to remove the masks only to find more distance and loneliness. Eventually it was not possible to connect to any part of her that was genuine because any aliveness, purity, clarity, purpose, love, truth etc. was buried so deep.

My personal struggle to live my truth has been difficult with minimal support from family, community or humanity at large. However, I have found a depth of aliveness, beauty, love and connectedness with the Ultimate Creator that is only possible when being true to myself. The journey of self-knowledge/self-realization is a process of un-veiling and bold courageous compassion for self and others. The process caused me to witness my own pain, sadness, insecurities, inadequacies as well as my own joy, pleasures, creativity, skills and abilities, self-perseverance, and the magnificence of the human spirit. I have come to know that heart - centred living is the only living worth living.

The journey to self has given me healing tools that I love to share with others so they too may dive deep within to navigate their inner territory and discover what is necessary for them to experience enormous joy, wonder, beauty and love within themselves and the world around them.

Contributed by **Tracey Farrell Munro,** Artist, Singer/Songwriter, Poet, Landscape Designer/Gardener www.creationsbytracey.com

Freedom

- I have discovered the secret that after climbing a great hill, one only finds that there are many more hills to climb....With freedom comes responsibilities, and I dare not linger, for my long walk is not yet ended *(Nelson Mandela, Long Walk to Freedom, 1995)*.

- For to be free is not merely to cast off one's chains, but to live in a way that respects and enhances the freedom of others *(Nelson Mandela, Long Walk to Freedom, 1995)*.

- Our march to freedom is irreversible. We must not allow fear to stand in our way *(Nelson Mandela, Our March to Freedom is Irreversible, 1990).*

- There is no easy walk to freedom anywhere, and many of us will have to pass through the valley of the shadow of death again and again before we reach the mountaintop of our desires *(Nelson Mandela, Long Walk to Freedom, 1995).*

- Though in reality there is no bondage, the individual is in bondage as long as there exists the feeling of limitation *(Tripurarahasya).*

- Freedom of choice is more to be treasured than any possession earth can give *(David Oman McKay, LDS General Conference Report, April 1950, page 32).*

- You are what your driving desire is. As your desire is, so is your will. As your will is, so is your deed. As your deed is, so is your destiny *(Brihadaranyaka Upanishad IV.4.5).*

True Life Story

by **Pastor Benjamin Wamalwa Khaemba**

"What we do in life, echoes in eternity"
- *Maximus, the Gladiator*

The Lord will make a way for all who have Faith and Hope in Him! In John 14:6, "Jesus saith unto him, I am the way, the truth, and the life."

We have nothing to fear and nothing to worry about when we keep our mind upon Him. There is not a more faithful person to depend on than the Lord. We cannot even depend on our own self, or our own opinions more than we depend on the Lord. He sees what we cannot see, and he can do what no other power can do.

We must daily put all our trust in the Lord, and He will make the way for us spiritually, physically, and financially. We must not worry and fret, but look to Jesus who is the author and finisher of our faith.

Faith in God will lift you above the doubts and fears of this life and give you evidence of things not yet seen. Faith knows that God will make the way no matter what it looks like to our human eyes. I am praying for anything we people may need in our hearts, and I am depending on the Lord to work all things out for our highest good. Believe with me and expect the Lord to make the way, "The effectual fervent prayer of a righteous man availed much." James 5:16

Contributed by: **Benjamin Wamalwa Khaemba,** Republic of Kenya, P.O. Box 354 Bungoma, Kenya 50200
khaembabenjamin@yahoo.com

Fountain of God's Grace Revival Ministries is a non-profit Christian organization founded by God's servant Benjamin Wamalwa Khaemba, who is called by God to preach and teach the word of Hope, Grace, and Encouragement, bringing nations into spiritual practice, for children in all areas of life ... in the spirit of Gladness and simplicity of Heart, by informing them to be Joyful in Hope, for in Hope we were saved. As a non-profit Christian organization, Fountain of God's Grace Revival Ministries' heart-beat is to bring Hope and Grace to the Hopeless in all areas of life.

Grief / Sadness / Sorrow / Loss

- Shed no tear! O shed no tear! The flower will bloom another year *(John Keats, Faery Songs, I, 1818)*.

- Between grief and nothing I will take grief *(William Faulkner, The Wild Palms, 1939)*.

- Truly, it is in darkness that one finds the light, so when we are in sorrow, then this light is nearest of all to us *(Meister Eckhart)*.

- Pip, dear old chap, life is made of ever so many partings welded together *(Charles Dickens, Great Expectations, 1860-1861, Ch. 27).*

- The pain of parting is nothing to the joy of meeting again *(Charles Dickens, Nicholas Nickleby, 1838-1839, Chapter 3).*

- Everything in life that we really accept undergoes a change. So suffering must become love. That is the mystery *(Katherine Mansfield, The Journal of Katherine Mansfield, 1927).*

- There is a land of the living and a land of the dead and the bridge is love, the only survival, the only meaning *(Thornton Wilder, The Bridge of San Luis Rey, 1927).*

- For certain is death for the born and certain is birth for the dead. Therefore do not grieve over what is inevitable *(Bhagavad Gita 2: 27).*

- Life does not cease to be funny when people die any more than it ceases to be serious when people laugh *(George Bernard Shaw, The Doctor's Dilemma, V, 1906).*

Infinity / Timelessness

- Life is real! Life is earnest!
  And the grave is not its goal;
  Dust thou art, to dust returnest,
  Was not spoken of the soul *(Henry Wadsworth Longfellow, A Psalm of Life, 1839, st. 2).*

- Shed no tear! O shed no tear!
  The flower will bloom another year *(John Keats, Faery Songs, I, 1818).*

- The Way that can be told is not the eternal Way. The name that can be named is not the eternal name *(Lao Tzu, Tao Te Ching 1).*

- The soul of man is immortal and imperishable *(Plato, Republic X: 608-D)*.

True Life Story: Pujya Gurudevshri Rakeshbhai

"Religion has only one answer and that is meditation.
And meditation means how to empty yourself."
   - OSHO

Forgiveness

What is forgiveness? Seeing others' faults, you feel compassionate rather than disturbed. You become like a flower that gives fragrance when crushed.

God provides food for every bird, but not in the nest. Pray with persistence, but never ever for favours. Day in and Day out, Plead to the Lord to make you pure.

When you are shown a fault, do not label yourself a complete failure. Know that there is just a patch to be worked upon. REALISE, do not React!

A devotee's barometer lies in his Guru's eyes! In there he reads failure, or progress and accordingly charts his way to success! Learn to appreciate others' view points. Each of us acts according to our point of view.

I AM A PEACEFUL, POWERFUL SOUL. I enact different roles. So what if I fail in one? So what if I win in one? All roles fade away, as an Eternal Witness, I STAY.

Success: Do what is right, in the right way, at the right time!

Tea in boiling water releases taste, colour and aroma. So too in difficulties, your virtues unfold.

Patience with family is love, Patience with others is respect, Patience with yourself is confidence, Patience with GOD is Faith.

Someday, somehow, whatever you prayed for will come true. It may not be in the exact package you wanted, but it will be what God thinks is best for you.

Contributed by **Pujya Gurudevshri Rakeshbhai**, Mumbai, India

Innocence / Child

- I still get wildly enthusiastic about little things... I play with leaves. I skip down the street and run against the wind *(Leo Buscaglia)*.

- There's no point in being grown-up if you can't be childish sometimes *(The Doctor, Doctor Who, "Robot")*.

- The smile that flickers on baby's lips when he sleeps— does anybody know where it was born? *(Rabindranath Tagore, Gitanjali, 1912, 61)*.

- Children are a wonderful gift. They have an extraordinary capacity to see into the heart of things and to expose sham and humbug for what they are *(Desmond Tutu, Believe: The Words and Inspiration of Desmond Tutu, 2007, p. 39)*.

- Children have the resilience to outlive their sufferings, if given a chance *(Ishmael Beah, The Long Way Gone: Memoirs of a Boy Soldier, 2008)*.

Joy / Bliss / Happiness / Satisfaction / Fulfillment

Original Quotes Contributed by Satish Kaku

"You will know your purpose in life once you know who you are."

"When your Soul separates from your head, or your head is replaced by heart, you get the new set of eyes and start seeing this Universe as a place of great abundance, choice, and opportunities. You will see things and people as they are at their core ... full of Love and Divinity."

"Ego does not come with love.
  Ego walks alone, and love
  Walks in Oneness."

Contributed by **Satish Kaku**
Studied at J.J. School of Arts
Mumbai, Maharashtra, India
http://facebook.com/kaku.satish
http://twitter.com/SatishKaku

Quotes about Joy/Happiness/Bliss

• Happiness is the absence of striving for happiness (*Chuang Tzu*).

• Happiness in this world, when it comes, comes incidentally. Make it the object of pursuit, and it leads us a wild-goose chase, and is never attained. Follow some other object, and very possibly we may find that we have caught happiness without dreaming of it (*Nathaniel Hawthorne, Notebooks, 1851*).

• What is the purpose of life? It is Joy *(Abraham-Hicks)*.

• Happiness is not achieved by the conscious pursuit of happiness; it is generally the by-product of other activities (*Aldous Huxley, Essay "Distractions I" in Vedanta for the Western World (1945) edited by Christopher Isherwood*).

- Caring about others, running the risk of feeling, and leaving an impact on people, brings happiness

(Harold Kushner).

- Always remember: happiness is not a side matter in your spiritual journey - it is essential *(Nachman of Breslov).*

- It is a great mitzvah (commandment) to always be happy *(Nachman of Breslov, LM2 34).*

- Laughter is the language of the soul - *La risa es el lenguaje del alma (Pablo Neruda).*

- I came from nowhere, made a mark. I am happy. Looking back there are no regrets *(Manisha Koirala).*

- So many people are waiting for their happiness to come. It's not here yet, but they are waiting. It's like standing in a line waiting for your bus. One day, people say, my ship will come. One day, I'll make it. One day, I'll be happy. Ships come and go, and they wait for theirs. They think about jumping on other people's ships. They think everything. Yet, incredibly enough, there has always been someone who has pointed out the simple fact that what we are looking for is inside *(Prem Rawat, Honolulu, Hawaii, December 4, 1991).*

- The more we have the less we own *(Meister Eckhart).*

Human happiness and human satisfaction must ultimately come from within oneself *(Dalai Lama, The Path to Tranquility: Daily Wisdom, 1998 edited by Renuka Singh).*

- Many people think that if they were only in some other place, or had some other job, they would be happy. Well, that is doubtful. So get as much happiness out of what you are doing as you can and don't put off being happy until some future date *(Dale Carnegie).*

- Therefore I tell you, do not worry about your life, what you will eat or drink; or about your body, what you will wear. Is not life more important than food, and the body more important than clothes? Look at the birds of the air; they do not sow or reap or store away in barns, and yet your heavenly Father feeds them. Are you not much more valuable than they? Who of you by worrying can add a single hour to his life? And why do you worry about clothes? See how the lilies of the field grow. They do not labour or spin. Yet I tell you that not even Solomon in all his splendour was dressed like one of these. *(Matthew 6: 25-30)*.

- Therefore do not worry about tomorrow, for tomorrow will worry about itself. Each day has enough trouble of its own *(Matthew 6: 34)*.

- Abiding joy comes to those who still the mind *(Bhagavad Gita 6:10)*.

- Not by a shower of gold coins does contentment arise in sensual pleasures *(Buddha, Dhammapada 186)*.

- Happiness is a good flow of life *(Zeno of Citium)*.

- Happy is the man that hath not walked in the counsel of the wicked or stood in the way of sinners, nor sat in the seat of the scornful. But his delight is in the law of the Lord *(Psalm 1:1-2)*.

- The LORD is my shepherd; I shall not want *(Psalm 23:1)*.

- Follow your bliss and don't be afraid, and doors will open where you never knew there were going to be a door *(Joseph Campbell with Bill Moyers, The Power of Myth, 1988)*.

- Many persons have a wrong idea of what constitutes true happiness. It's not attained through self-gratification, but through fidelity to a worthy purpose *(Helen Keller, The Simplest Way to be Happy, 1933)*.

Meditation / Awareness / Reflection

Original Quote by Onkar Singh
"*Everything you would want is right within yourself*"
- **Onkar Singh**

This is the greatest insight that I've learned in this lifetime.

Onkar Singh
Naturopathic Physician
Brantford, Ontario (Canada)
www.ndoc.ca

Meditation / Awareness / Reflection

- The ordinary surroundings of life which are esteemed by men (as their actions testify) to be the highest good, may be classed under the three heads — Riches, Fame, and the Pleasures of Sense: with these three the mind is so absorbed that it has little power to reflect on any different good *(Baruch Spinoza, On the Improvement of the Understanding, 1662, Pt. I, 3)*. That which cannot be expressed by speech, but by which speech is expressed—That alone known as Brahman and not that which people here worship. That which cannot be apprehended by the mind, but by which, they say, the mind is apprehended—That alone known as Brahman and not that which people here worship. That which cannot be perceived by the eye, but by which the eye is perceived—That alone known as Brahman and not that which people here worship. That which cannot he heard by the ear, but by which the hearing is perceived—That alone known as Brahman and not that which people here worship *(Kena Upanishad 1:5-8)*.

- Two birds, united always and known by the same name, closely cling to the same tree. One of them eats the sweet fruit but the other looks on without eating. When the first beholds the other, she then becomes free from grief *(Mundaka Upanishad 3.1.1-2)*.

- It is because everyone under heaven recognizes beauty as beauty that the idea of ugliness exists *(Lao Tzu, Tao Te Ching 2)*.

- Without knowledge of self there is no knowledge of God *(John Calvin, Institutio Christianae Religionis, 1559)*.

- There is a difference between knowing the path and walking the path *(Morpheus, The Matrix)*.

- It is the world that has been pulled over your eyes to blind you from the truth *(Morpheus, The Matrix)*.

- Once upon a time, I, Chuang Tzu, dreamt I was a butterfly, fluttering hither and thither, a veritable butterfly, enjoying itself to the full of its bent, and not knowing it was Chuang Chou. Suddenly I awoke, and came to myself, the veritable Chuang Chou. *Now* I do not know whether it was then I dreamt I was a butterfly, or whether I am now a butterfly dreaming I am a man. Between me and the butterfly there must be a difference. This is an instance of transformation *(Chuang Tzu, Zhuangzi quoted in The Three Religions of China: Lectures Delivered at Oxford (1913) by William Edward Soothill, p. 75)*.

Peace / Contentment / Silence / Equanimity / Inner Guidance

True Life Story by Vicky Mac Lean

"One does not need buildings, money, power, or status to practice the Art of Peace. Heaven is right where you are standing, and that is the place to train."
- **Moribei Ueshiba**
  December 14, 1883 – April 26th, 1969

The quote above comes from Moribei Ueshiba, the founder of modern Aikido, in "Osensei" or Great Teacher and can be found in his wonderful book *The Art of Peace*, a collection of inspirational teachings and insights, showing that the real 'Way of the Warrior' is a path of compassion, love, wisdom and fearlessness, a true discipline of Mind, Body, and Spirit, non-violence leading to victory over conflict.

Such a quote applies entirely to the whole philosophy of life in that we need to succeed and find contentment ... and peace already lies within us, that Divine spark that connects us to all life and the Universe. We are all one and by training ourselves in this thought process we *manifest the abundance and peace that the Universe bestows on all of us if we are prepared to listen.*

I came across this teaching through my late husband Dr. Leslie Mac Lean an 8th Dan in Aikido and numerous other Japanese martial arts Dan graduates. He lived for a time in Japan whilst training at the Kodokan Institute for Judo. It was finally through Aikido and the Philosophy that comes with this gentle art introduced to him by Kenshio Abbe 10th Dan, that my husband began to understand that *a soft step and an open hand* achieve far more than grasping for power, money, or position.

These beliefs mirror my own experience of the practice of Reiki, which also becomes a philosophy and life path.

I have used the little book **The Art of Peace** as a daily reflection, opening the pages at random to provide a 'thought' for the day. Wisdom and gentle grace continue to help and inspire me, and during those last few months of my husband's illness those words sustained me, and I placed this book with him on his final journey home. We all need to walk the path of the Warrior at times and I can think of no finer guide than Osensei.

- Contributed by **Vicky Mac Lean**
  Coventry, U.K.
  Reiki Master Teacher
  Usui Shiki Ryoho and Nemeton Reiki
  www.tendairyu.webs.com

Quotes about Peace / Contentment / Silence / Equanimity / Inner Guidance

- A crust eaten in peace is better than a banquet partaken in anxiety *(Aesop, The Town Mouse and the Country Mouse)*.

- All God wants of man is a peaceful heart *(Meister Eckhart)*.

- When you lose touch with inner stillness, you lose touch with yourself. When you lose touch with yourself, you lose yourself in the world *(Eckhart Tolle, A New Earth, 2005)*.

- I have never felt that anything really mattered but the satisfaction of knowing that you stood for the things in which you believed and had done the very best you could *(Eleanor Roosevelt, My Day, 8 November 1944)*.

- It isn't enough to talk about peace. One must believe in it. And it isn't enough to believe in it. One must work at it *(Eleanor Roosevelt, Voice of America broadcast, 11 November 1951)*.

- Peace is inside you. Wherever you go, peace goes with you *(Prem Rawat, Addressing faculty and guests at the Indian Institute of Technology [IIT], New Delhi, November 7, 2004)*.

God grant me the serenity
to accept the things I cannot change,
courage to change the things I can,
and the wisdom to know the difference
- *(Reinhold Niebuhr, The Serenity Prayer, 1942)*.

- If everyone demanded peace instead of another television set, then there'd be peace *(John Lennon, Guitar Player, 1 August 2004)*.

- Peace is inside you. Wherever you go, peace goes with you *(Prem Rawat, Addressing faculty and guests at the Indian Institute of Technology [IIT], New Delhi, November 7, 2004)*.

- The first to be summoned to Paradise on the Day of Resurrection will be those who praise God in prosperity and adversity *(Prophet Muhammad, Al-Tirmidhi, Hadith 730)*.

- Be governed by your internal compass, not by some clock on the wall *(Stephen Covey)*.

- Nothing is miserable but what is thought so, and contrariwise, every estate is happy if he that bears it be content *(Boethius, The Consolation of Philosophy, Book II, section 4, line 64)*.

- If you cannot get things as much as you desire then be contented with what you have *(Imam Ali)*.

- Be content with your lot; one cannot be first in everything *(Aesop, Juno and the Peacock)*.

- To achieve peace, patterns of fear, resentment, mistrust and indifference to the suffering of others must be broken *(King Abdullah of Jordan, "A responsibility to make peace'," International Herald Tribune, 21 June 2006)*.

- *Reality is apparent when one ceases to compare.* — There is "what is" only when there is no comparison at all, and to live with what is, is to be *peaceful (Bruce Lee, Striking Thoughts, 2000, p. 19)*.

- Without going out of my door
  I can know all things on earth
  Without looking out of my window
  I can know the ways of Heaven

  The farther one travels
  The less one knows....
  Arrive without travelling
  See all without looking
  Do all without doing *(The Beatles, "The Inner Light")*.

- When anger rises, think of the consequences *(Confucius)*.

- Better a dry crust with peace and quiet than a house full of feasting with strife *(Proverbs 17:1)*.

- The Lord is all peace, all virtue and all wealth; remembering Him, all misery and hunger depart *(Guru Ram Das, Guru Granth Sahib, 493:11)*.

- By remaining silent, inner silence is not obtained, even by remaining continuously absorbed in meditation *(Guru Nanak, Guru Granth Sahib, 1-5)*.

- When all the senses are stilled, when the mind is at rest, when the intellect wavers not- then, say the wise, is reached the highest state. This calm of the senses and the mind has been defined as yoga. One who attains it is freed from delusion *(Katha Upanishad 2.6.10-11)*.

- Just as a deep lake is clear and still, even so, on hearing the teachings and realizing them, the wise become exceedingly peaceful *(Buddha, Dhammapada 82)*.

- The monk looks for peace within himself, and not in any other place *(Sutta Nipata 919-20)*.

- Better than a thousand useless words is one useful word, hearing which one attains peace *(The Buddha, Dhammapada 100)*.

- Nothing real can be threatened. Nothing unreal exists. Herein lies the peace of God

(A Course in Miracles, 2007, p. x).

- Even the ignorant may appear very worthy, If they keep silent before the learned *(Tiruvalluvar, Tirukkural Verse XLI.3)*.

- In peace sons bury fathers, but in war fathers bury sons *(Herodotus, Histories I: 87)*.

- And he shall judge among many people, and rebuke strong nations afar off; and they shall beat their swords into ploughshares, and their spears into pruning-hooks: nation shall not lift up a sword against nation; neither shall they learn war any more *(Micah 4:3)*.

- Don't fight for peace. Peace will come naturally *(Huai-nan Tzu)*.

- Let silence be your general rule, or say only what is necessary and in few words *(Epictetus, Golden Sayings of Epictetus 164)*.

- Peace comes from being able to contribute the best that we have, and all that we are, toward creating a world that supports everyone *(Hafsat Abiola, Architects of Peace, 2000)*.

- Violence is unnecessary and costly. Peace is the only way *(Julius Nyerere quoted in Quotes about Peace by Richard M. Nixon, p. 17)*.

- What we need is a generation of peace *(Jawaharlal Nehru quoted in Quotes about Peace by Richard M. Nixon, p. 17)*.

- Though force can protect in emergency, only justice, fairness, consideration and cooperation can finally lead men to the dawn of eternal peace *(Dwight D. Eisenhower)*.

- Even when a person who is poor in spirit desires something and doesn't get it, they are at peace because they know that things do not bring happiness. The depth of their spirit is with God and they possess a sense of serenity *(Mother Angelica as quoted in Mother Angelica's Little Book of Life Lessons and Everyday Spirituality. By Raymond Arroyo, 2008, p. 39)*.

Purpose / Mission / Values / Ethics

True Life Story/Quote by Ed Woods

I worked at a large media corporation with our building run by unethical and unfeeling management. Rumours of a layoff were rampant for a long time and management tried every tactic to harass staff into quitting which would save them millions because the plan secretly involved thousands of unsuspecting employees.

My supervisor was running an outside based theft-to-order ring and any employee who purchased from him would have a great employee file, but those who didn't, such as I, were consistently targeted for abuse. I was the only employee who stood up to him and the director who was stealing computers from our storage area to run a home-based internet server. It was a difficult task but I did not back down from either one of these two.

One day I was called to a meeting and a co-worker was to assist me with the agenda and as we walked upstairs to the third floor boardroom he stated that the meeting was on the second floor instead. As we moved down the hallway to the storage, which was considerably large, I asked them why they were holding it in this dump of a room. At the doorway he stayed in place, and once inside the room I could see my general manager and a stranger standing by an old, broken card table with bent, metal fold-away legs and the old plywood seated chairs.

I laughed and said, "Gee, I wonder what is going on in this splendid motif?" I was told to sit down but declined and said, "Hey, I have looked for a job before so let me sign the 'Hit List' papers and get out of here."

They said that the lay-off notice must be read out loud as a procedure to which I replied: "You mean you want to twist the knife in my back as personal entertainment before throwing me across the property line."

When they finished, I asked; "Why could you not do this with class and use the boardroom upstairs?" I received no response them. As I left the room while they wished me good luck with my future, I turned and stated: "You know you solved my problems of working in this poison pit and remember:"

"'If people are judged by the company they keep then a company should be judged by the people they keep.'"

While I was no longer working there, I felt proud of my values. I held my head high as I walked away to never look back.
- Contributed by **Ed Woods,** Executive Member, Tower Poetry Society, Hamilton, Ontario (Canada) www.towerpoetry.ca

Quotes: Purpose / Mission / Values / Ethics / Goals

- I felt called to write about certain values, such as integrity and commitment, faith and forgiveness, about the virtues of simplicity, about the difference between "amusing ourselves to death" and finding meaningful pleasures—even joy *(Sidney Poitier, The Measure of a Man, 2000)*.

- One day, my mother said to me, "If you become a soldier, you will be a general; if you become a monk you'll end up as the pope." Instead, I became a painter and now I am Picasso *(Pablo Picasso)*.

- Move on up towards your destination

    though you may find from time to time complications *(Curtis Mayfield, "Move On Up," Curtis)*.

- Many persons have a wrong idea of what constitutes true happiness. It is not attained through self-gratification but through fidelity to a worthy purpose *(Helen Keller, The Simplest Way to be Happy, 1933*

- I am not sick. I am broken. But I am happy to be alive as long as I can paint *(Frida Kahlo, Time Magazine, "Mexican Autobiography," 1953-04-27)*.

- Whatever moral rules you have deliberately proposed to yourself, abide by them as they were laws, and as if you would be guilty of impiety by violating any of them. Don't regard what anyone says of you, for this, after all, is no concern of yours *(Epictetus, The Enchiridion, 50)*.

- Nothing can bring you peace but the triumph of principles *(Ralph Waldo Emerson, Self-reliance)*.

- There is a higher court than courts of justice and that is the court of conscience. It supersedes all other courts *(Mahatma Gandhi)*.

- You cannot adhere to the teachings of the church on Sunday and not apply to the marketplace on Monday *(LeRoy Bailey Jr., From sermon: He Is Lord)*.

- Evil deeds do not prosper as the slow man catches up with the swift *(Homer, The Odyssey, VIII, I: 329)*.

- What you do not want done to yourself, do not do it to others *(Confucius, Analects 15: 23)*.

- Two things cause people to be destroyed: fear of poverty and seeking superiority through pride *(Imam Ali, Majlisi, Bihārul Anwār, v. 72, p.39)*.

- The impurity of the mind produces greed, and the impurity of the tongue produces falsehood. The impurity of the eyes is to gaze upon the beauty of another's spouse and his or her wealth. The impurity of the ears is to listen to the slander of others *(Guru Nanak, Guru Granth Sahib 472: 16-17)*.

- We are to live so that no harm or pain is caused by our thoughts, words or deeds to any other being *(Patanjali as quoted in Wisdom for the Soul by Larry Chang, 2006, p. 136).*

- That which is hateful to you, do not do to your neighbour. That is the whole Torah; the rest is the explanation. Go and study it *(Hillel the Elder, Babylonian Talmud Shabbat 31a).*
- Father and mother should be respected and so should elders, kindness to living beings should be made strong and the truth should be spoken *(Ashoka the Great, Quotes from Edicts).*

- What you get by achieving your goals is not as important as what you become by achieving your goals *(Zig Ziglar).*

- A goal is not always meant to be reached, it often serves simply as something to aim at *(Bruce Lee, Striking Thoughts, 2000, p. 121).*

Self-worth / Self-esteem / Confidence

True Life Story by Jennifer Vermeer

"Paint yourself a picture of what you wish you looked like
Maybe then they just might feel an ounce of your pain
Come into focus step out of the shadows it's a losing battle
There's no need to be ashamed
Cause they don't even know all they see is scars
They don't see the angel living in your heart
Let them find the real you buried deep within
Let them know with all you've got
that you are not your skin"
   -   Lyric excerpt from the song SKIN, by Sixx A.M. band

I have battled with self –esteem issues all my life, first because I was never the pretty girl, and later in my adult life with weight issues. It is amazing how cruel people can be. I learned quickly, especially in the circle I travelled in, mostly musicians, that the woman was viewed for one reason, because she was *sexy*. I was cool to hang with, but never considered *sexy* enough to be on their arms, at least not in public.

It wasn't until I became an adult and stopped chasing *band boys* that I found a bit of self-esteem, but the sadness of feeling *not pretty* stayed with me. I may have stopped loving *band boys,* but I never stopped loving music, and when my favourite artist released the song *SKIN,* my first listen through brought me to full out sobbing tears, I cried for a long time. I felt like it was written about me, and since the release of this song, I hold my head higher and love myself more. Seems silly that a song could start to repair me, but the truth is it went a long way to undoing all the damage I let others do to me. It also went a long way to teach me that judgement is something we should never do to each other as a society; everyone has their own inner demons they are fighting with. Why make them worse by pointing your finger just to make yourself feel better in the moment? In the long run you will only be doing more damage to yourself.
- **Jennifer Vermeer,** Hamilton, Ontario (Canada) Mother of Nicholas, the love of my life. Significant other and my best friend, Chris. *Hairstylist* for Maddison Avenue, Hamilton, Ontario, Canada

Quotes on Self-worth / Self-esteem / Confidence

- The secret of life is that I have validated my existence. I know that I am worth more than my house, my bank account, or any physical thing *(Carlos Santana).*

- First, we must massively assert our dignity and worth. We must stand up amidst a system that still oppresses us and develop an unassailable and majestic sense of values *(Martin Luther King, Jr., Where do We Go From Here?, 1967).*

- The secret of life is that I have validated my existence. I know that I am worth more than my house, my bank account, or any physical thing *(Carlos Santana).*

- Do exactly what you would do if you felt most secure *(Meister Eckhart).*

- Hobbes: So the secret to good self-esteem is to lower your expectations to the point where they're already met?

(The Days are Just Packed p23).

- Respect yourself and others will respect you *(Confucius).*

- Never esteem anything as of advantage to you that will make you break your word or lose your self-respect *(Marcus Aurelius, Meditations III: 7).*

- Self-love, my liege, is not so vile a sin as self-neglecting *(William Shakespeare, Henry V, II: iv, 1599).*

- When you cannot get a compliment any other way, pay yourself one *(Mark Twain as quoted in 20,000 Quips & Quotes by Evan Esar, 1995, p. 164).*

- To love oneself is the beginning of a life-long romance *(Oscar Wilde, An Ideal Husband, 1895).*

- The curious paradox is that when I accept myself just as I am, then I can change *(Carl Rogers quoted in Sunbeams: A Book of Quotations, Sy Safransky, 1990, p. 101).*

- Once you get rid of the idea that you must please other people before you please yourself, and you begin to follow your own instincts – only then can you be successful *(Raquel Welch quoted in The Balanced Mom by Brian Simpson, 2006, p. 85).*

- When we really love and accept and approve of ourselves exactly as we are, then everything in life works *(Louise Hay, You Can Heal Your Life, 2009, p. 19).*

- We, each of us, need so much to be affirmed. For each of us has – gnawing away at the center of our being – a sense of insecurity, some more than others. And frequently, the more insecure, the more aggressive we become *(Desmond Tutu, Interview at Academy of Achievement, 12 June 2004)*.

- Love yourself, appreciate yourself, see the good in you, see the God in you, and respect yourself *(Betty Shabazz quoted in Wisdom for the Soul by Larry Chang, 2006, p. 43)*.

- Love yourself first and everything else falls into line. You really have to love yourself to get anything done in this world *(Lucille Ball as quoted in The Now Age by Zsuzsana Summer, 2004, p. 117)*.

- His own image; no longer a dark, gray bird, ugly and disagreeable to look at, but a graceful and beautiful swan. To be born in a duck's nest, in a farmyard, is of no consequence to a bird, if it is hatched from a swan's egg *(Hans Christian Anderson, The Ugly Duckling, 1932)*.

Spontaneity / Opportunity / Flexibility

- When one door of happiness closes, another opens; but often we look so long at the closed door that we do not see the one which has been opened for us *(Helen Keller, We Bereaved, 1929)*.

- Analysis kills spontaneity. The grain once ground into flour springs and germinates no more *(Henri Frederic Amiel)*.

- One should be in harmony with, not in opposition to, the strength and force of the opposition. This means that one should do nothing that is not natural or spontaneous; the important thing is not to strain in any way *(Bruce Lee, Striking Thoughts, 2000, p. 20)*.

- If you remove the veil that separate souls, you will see that in reality only the One exists. Duality is only owing to the squint of your eyes *(Sultan Bahu, Risala-e-Roohi)*..

- A very great vision is needed and the man who has it must follow it as the eagle seeks the deepest blue of the sky *(Crazy Horse)*.

- This must be a world of democracy and respect for human rights, a world freed from the horrors of poverty, hunger, deprivation and ignorance, relieved of the threat and the scourge of civil wars and external aggression and unburdened of the great tragedy of millions forced to become refugees *(Nelson Mandela, Nobel Prize acceptance speech, 1993)*.

- Imagine there's no countries,
  It isn't hard to do,
  Nothing to kill or die for,
  No religion too,
  Imagine all the people
  living life in peace...

  You may say I'm a dreamer,
  but I'm not the only one,
  I hope someday you'll join us,
  And the world will be as one *(John Lennon, "Imagine," 1971)*.

- It's really a wonder that I haven't dropped all my ideals, because they seem so absurd and impossible to carry out. Yet I keep them, because in spite of everything I still believe that people are really good at heart *(Anne Frank, The Diary, 15 July 1944)*.

- Everyone needs to be valued. Everyone has the potential to give something back *(Diana, Princess of Wales, The Guardian, December 9, 1995, p. 2)*.

- Man is not entirely an animal. He aspires to a spiritual vision, which is the vision of the whole truth *(Rabindranath Tagore, Gitanjali, 1912)*.

Wholeness / Oneness / Unity

True Life Story on Unity by Anthony Monaco

Lyric verse from: **HAPPY XMAS (WAR IS OVER)**
John Lennon / Yoko Ono

"War is over if you want it, war is over now."

The quote from the lyric verse "Happy Xmas (War is Over), by John Lennon / Yoko Ono, is my favourite quote since I do believe that *war is over now.* We just have to realize this truth within us to have the reality of *peace* become a living experience.

Peace

Some of my further insights on peace are as follows:

"Education is the key to world peace. This truth should be grasped and acted upon. I do not really accept to be in any particular group who is against another group. This just causes war. I take the stand of peace and try to bring peace to these warring factions being with both or neither ... being with peace. And if one group or many also take a stand for peace, and try to bring peace to these warring factions, being with both or neither ... being with peace ... If one group or many also take a stand for peace, and come to understand creation ... I would be happy to see progress in the bettering of society, and increasing the standard of living through human relations."

Unity and Peace

Concerning the state of the world we live in - as beautiful as this planet and all its inhabitants are, both wonderful and a part of a larger unity - this unity between the individual and the non-dualistic state of eternity, has through the ages, become more and more *less* apparent in the human race. We have become greedy and envious in our actions, due to misunderstanding of our surroundings and how we compare our individual self to the larger creation. We have forgotten the true nature of the part we play in all of creation and have been conditioned, sheltered from the Truth. Whenever I have returned to my ideals intuitively, respectably, with thoughts of unity, then I would find inner peace in my life. From my personal experiences, I feel that peace attained through a comprehension of Unity is the goal of humanity. Through Unity our society would find greater strength; through the strength and wisdom found in various traditions and cultures around the world and in our own nation. Unity would lead to greater freedom, harmony understanding between people and nations. Unity would include humanity and extend out into creation, providing a sense of balance and a sense of individuality based on our shared bonds.

Creativity

"I find creativity a doorway to spirituality and a bridge over time and space to a crest of subconscious becoming. To me creativity is one of the best ways to reach understandings of nature, and nature is in its essence built of creative forces. I am always experimenting with new, creative possibilities such as photography, leaded glass, guitar, and most importantly writing. I believe in the ways of peace, and peace awareness. I also believe in the evolution of mankind into a utopian existence of understanding the creative nature of the universe. The effect of war due to human depression and misguidance goes against humankind."

- Contributed by **Anthony Monaco** Hamilton, ON www3.sympatico.ca/anthonymonaco

Wholeness / Oneness / Unity

"You have noticed that everything an Indian does is in a circle, and that is because the Power of the World always works in circles."

(Black Elk as quoted in *Native American Wisdom* by Edward S. Curtis, 1993, p.20).

- They that be whole need not a physician, but they that are sick (Matthew 9:12).

- I have a dream that my four little children will one day live in a nation where they will not be judged by the colour of their skin but by the content of their character *(Martin Luther King, Jr., I Have a Dream, 1963)*.

- We might have our differences, but we are one people with a common destiny in our rich variety of culture, race and tradition *(Nelson Mandela, ANC Victory Speech, 1994)*.

- I want you to be concerned about your next door neighbour. Do you know your next door neighbour?

(Mother Theresa).

- Even as the fingers of the two hands are equal, so are human beings equal to one another *(Prophet Muhammad, Final Sermon, 10 A.H. or 630 A.D.)*.

- More than anything, it is that sense- that despite great differences in wealth, we rise and fall together

(Barack Obama, The Audacity of Hope, 2006, p.193).

- Our individual salvation depends on collective salvation. Because thinking only about yourself, fulfilling your immediate wants and needs, betrays a poverty of ambition *(Barack Obama, Wesleyan Graduation Ceremony, Middletown, Connecticut, May 25, 2008)*

They all need to be reassured that there is so much to be gained by reaching out to others; that diversity is indeed a strength and not a *threat (Queen Elizabeth II, A plea for increased tolerance and understanding in her Christmas Day Broadcast, 2004)*.

- Now I've been crying lately, thinking about the world as it is. Why must we go on hating, why can't we live in bliss? *(Cat Stevens [Yusuf Islam] Teaser and the Firecat, 1971, "Peace Train").*

- In this increasingly interdependent world in which we live in we have an obligation to explore areas of convergence *(Manmohan Singh).*

- The web of our life is of a mingled yarn, good and ill together *(William Shakespeare, All's Well That Ends Well, Act IV).*

- I have cherished the ideal of a democratic and free society in which all persons will live together in harmony and with equal opportunities. It is an ideal which I hope to live for. But, my lord, if needs be, it is an ideal for which I am prepared to die *(Nelson Mandela, I am Prepared to Die, Pretoria Supreme Court, 20 April 1964).*

- If we cannot end now our differences, at least we can make the world safe for diversity. For, in the final analysis, our most basic common link is that we all inhabit this small planet. We all breathe the same air. We all cherish our children's future. And we are all mortal *(John F. Kennedy, Address at American University, Washington D.C., 10 June 1963).*

- Today, with globalization bringing us ever closer together, if we choose to ignore the insecurities of some, they will soon become the insecurities of all *(Mohamed ElBaradei, Nobel lecture, 2005).*

- Today, we are truly a global family. What happens in one part of the world may affect us all *(Dalai Lama, Nobel Lecture, 1989).*

- Humans are amphibians — half spirit and half animal.... As spirits they belong to the eternal world, but as animals they inhabit time *(C.S. Lewis, The Screwtape Letters, 1942).*

- Taoist philosophy ... is essentially monistic. ... Matter and energy, Yang and Yin, heaven and earth, are conceived of as essentially one or as two coexistent poles of one indivisible whole *(Bruce Lee, Striking Thoughts, 2000, p. 23)*.

- Rich and poor have this in common: The Lord is the Maker of them all *(Proverbs 22:2)*.

- O humankind! We have created you male and female, and have made you nations and tribes that you may know one another *(Quran 49:13)*.

- All this is Brahman. This Self too is Brahman *(Mandukya Upanishad 1:2-5)*.

- O Svetaketu, the great conclusion to which you come by the analysis of the three elements is the existence of pure Being as the background of all that exists *(Chandogya Upanishad 6.8.7)*.

- To the seer, all things have verily become the Self: what delusion, what sorrow, can there be for him who beholds that oneness? *(Isa Upanishad 7)*

- One discovers the common values of every culture, capable of uniting and not dividing *(Pope John Paul II)*.

- As we learn about each other so we learn about ourselves *(The First Doctor, Doctor Who in "The Edge of Destruction")*.

- But if we can't live together--We're gonna die alone *(Jack Shephard, Lost in "White Rabbit," 1.5)*.

- All things are implicated with one another, and the bond is holy; and there is hardly anything unconnected with any other thing *(Marcus Aurelius, Meditations VII: 9)*.

- There is one intelligent soul, though it seems to be divided *(Marcus Aurelius, Meditations XII: 30)*.

- You cannot conceive the many without the one *(Plato, Parmenides 166)*.

- Why should we consider woman less or inferior, when from her are born leaders and rulers? A woman alone gives birth to a daughter. Without her there can be no human birth *(Guru Nanak, Guru Granth Sahib, p. 473)*.

- I very much believe that we share the same human values *(Mohamed ElBaradei, Breaking the Cycle interview, 2003)*.

- Tear down the mosque and the temple too, break all that divides. But do not break the human heart as it is there that God resides *(Bulleh Shah)*.

- Human beings are members of a whole in creation of one essence and soul. If one member is afflicted and in pain, others members will feel troubled *(Saadi)*.

YOGA SPIRITUAL MASTERS

SWAMI SIVANANDA (Swami Vishnudevananda's Spiritual Master)
"There is something good in all seeming failures. You are not to see that now. Time will reveal it. Be patient."
"Put your heart, mind, and soul into even your smallest acts. This is the secret of success."
"Life is short. Time is fleeting. Realize the Self. Purity of the heart is the gateway to God. Aspire. Renounce. Meditate. Be good, do good. Be kind, be compassionate. Inquire, know Thyself."
"The real progress of the aspirant is measured by the extent to which he achieves inner tranquility."
"Your duty is to treat everybody with love as a manifestation of the Lord."
"An optimist sees an opportunity in every difficulty. A pessimist sees a difficulty in every opportunity."

SWAMI VISHNUDEVANANDA (Swami Swaroopananda's Spiritual Master)

"Real peace comes only to those who control the body and mind with self-discipline."

"An ounce of practice is worth a pound of theory."

"Health is wealth, peace of mind is happiness, Yoga shows the way."

SWAMI SWAROOPANANDA (Spiritual Director Sivananda Ashram, Paradise Island Nassau Bahamas)

"The time to learn to live together is upon us."

"Through multiplicity we eventually discover the underlying unity; we bathe in the love and Grace of God as we celebrate the unity in our diversity."

"I believe that there is never a better time than now for us to make vigorous efforts to break barriers."

SHAMBHU DAS (Professor of Music, University of Toronto, Canada, first & foremost disciple of Ravi Shankar)

"Through music I try to reach God. It is my goal."

"My music is my life."

"How can anyone possibly find a few moments of peace and relaxation in such a chaotic world? There are many paths naturally, however one of the most simple and accessible to all individuals is music."

AIR

Psychological Quotes – Chapter 2

The Psychological domain is connected to your Mind, to all your abilities that influence your thoughts along positive or negative channels. Through transformation of your beliefs and thought patterns, you want to develop good character. Psychological development and growth is a concern of positive thinking. You can reflect on the quotes in this chapter and consider the wisdom, knowledge and insights offered by them.

René Descartes had asserted "I think, therefore I am." What if we turn that around: "I am, therefore I think." Thought then becomes a partner with our consciousness, not something removed. You can become aware of consciousness through meditation, silence and placing your focus and attention on the present moment.

Positive thinking, optimism and the right attitude are essential to your psychological growth as evident from the True Life Stories contained in this chapter. So also is a clear and peaceful mind as Marcus Aurelius indicates:

"By a tranquil mind I mean nothing else than a mind well ordered" *(Meditations IV: 3).*

Attention / Focus / Present Moment

- I know for sure that what we dwell on is who we become *(Oprah Winfrey, O Magazine).*

- Look not mournfully into the Past. It comes not back again. Wisely improve the Present. It is thine *(Henry Wadsworth Longfellow, Hyperion, Bk. IV, Ch. 8, 1839).*

- *The Moment is freedom.* — I couldn't live by a rigid schedule. I try to live freely from moment to moment, letting things happen and adjusting to them *(Bruce Lee, Striking Thoughts, 2000, p. 13)*.

- Learn to become still and take your attention away from what you don't want and all the emotional charge around it and place the attention on what you wish to experience *(Rev. Michael Beckwith, The Secret [film])*.

- This instant is the only time there is

(A Course in Miracles, 2007, p. xi).

- All we have to decide is what to do with the time that is given us – Gandalf *(The Fellowship of the Ring, p. 432)*.

- Look not mournfully into the Past. It comes not back again. Wisely improve the Present. It is thine *(Henry Wadsworth Longfellow, Hyperion IV: 8)*.

- With thoughts fixed on the chosen target, that and that alone should be pursued *(Shantideva, The Way of the Boddhisattva, 2008, p. 111)*.

Belief

- The true basis of religion is not belief, but intuitive experience

(Paramhansa Yogananda, The Essence of Self-Realization).

When you believe in a thing, believe in it all the way, implicitly and unquestionably *(Walt Disney, Perceive This! : How to Get Everything You Want Out of Life by Changing Your Perceptions (2004) by Kevin A. Martin, Ch. 9, No Bar Too High!, p. 64)*.

- People believe willingly what they wish *(Julius Caesar, De Bello Gallico I: 1)*.

- There are no limitations to the self except those you believe in *(Jane Roberts, The Nature of Personal Reality, 1974)*.

- We are so much stronger than we imagine, and belief is one of the most valiant and long-lived human characteristics *(Lance Armstrong, It's Not About the Bike, 2000)*.

Character / Virtue / Dignity

- Character, not circumstances, makes the man *(Booker T. Washington, "Democracy and Education", speech, Institute of Arts and Sciences, Brooklyn NY, 1896-09-30)*.

- Knowledge will give you power, but character respect *(Bruce Lee, Striking Thoughts, 2000, p. 46)*.

- The most important thing for a young man is to establish a credit... a reputation, character *(John D. Rockefeller)*.

- Character is destiny *(Heraclitus, On the Universe, Fragment 121)*.

- Good character is not formed in a week or a month. It is created little by little, day by day. Protracted and patient effort is needed to develop good character *(Heraclitus)*.

- The example of great and pure characters is the only thing that can produce fine ideas and noble deeds *(Albert Einstein, The World As I See It, 1949)*.

- That is not riches, which may be lost; virtue is our true good and the true reward of its possessor *(Leonardo da Vinci, The Notebooks of Leonardo da Vinci, Translator Jean Paul Richter, 1888, XIX)*.

- Our life evokes our character and you find out more about yourself as you go on *(Joseph Campbell and The Power of Myth with Bill*

Moyers PBS television series, Mystic Fire Video, 2001, Episode 1, Chapter 12).

- The achievement of the hero is one that he is ready for and it's really a manifestation of his character *(Joseph Campbell and The Power of Myth with Bill Moyers PBS television series, Mystic Fire Video, 2001, Episode 1, Chapter 12).*

- Calvin: Nothing spoils fun like finding out it builds character *Attack of the Deranged Mutant Killer Monster Snow Goons p9).*

- It takes 20 years to build a reputation and five minutes to ruin it. If you think about that, you'll do things differently *(Warren Buffet).*

- Fine words and an insinuating appearance are seldom associated with true virtue *(Confucius, Analects 1: 3).*

- Character is much easier kept than recovered *(Thomas Paine, The American Crisis, 1925, p. 177).*

- To live each day as if it were your last – never agitated, never lazy, never a deceitful word – this is the path to the perfection of character *(Marcus Aurelius, Meditations 7: 69).*

- Character is like a tree and reputation like a shadow. The shadow is what we think of it; the tree is the real thing *(Abraham Lincoln as quoted in The Power of Reputation by Chris Komisarjevsky, 2012, p. 9).*

- Be more concerned with your character than your reputation, because your character is what you really are, while your reputation is merely what others think you are *(John Wooden, Beyond Success, 2001, p. 38).*

- Character makes life immortal. It survives even death *(Satya Sai Baba, Prema Vahini, posted on web Dec. 20, 1999 at* http://askbaba.helloyou.ch/premavahini/index.html*).*

- We do not attract what we want, but what we are *(James Allen, As a Man Thinketh, 1902)*.

Imagination / Dreaming

- Somehow, I can't believe that there are any heights to be scaled by a man who knows the secret of making dreams come true (Walt Disney, *Perceive This! : How to Get Everything You Want Out of Life by Changing Your Perceptions* (2004) *by Kevin A. Martin, Ch. 9, No Bar Too High!, p. 64)*.

- The key to realizing a dream is to focus not on success but significance - and then even the small steps and little victories along your path will take on greater meaning *(Oprah Winfrey, O Magazine, September 2002)*.

- When the jiva is overcome by light he sees no dreams; at that time, in this body, arises this happiness *(Prashna Upanishad 4:6)*.

- Dream as if you'll live forever. Live as if you'll die today *(James Dean as quoted in James Dean by Karen Clemens Warrick, 2006, p. 137)*.

- To dream big doesn't necessarily mean to imagine becoming the biggest movie star in the world. Dreaming big is about taking the simplest thing in life and enjoying it — and seeing it as the biggest thing that can possibly exist *(Salma Hayek, Interview with Oprah Winfrey in O magazine, "Passion," September 2003)*.

- We are so captivated by and entangled in our subjective consciousness that we have forgotten the age-old fact that God speaks chiefly through dreams and visions *(Carl Jung)*.

- All human beings are also dream beings. Dreaming ties all mankind together *(Jack Kerouac, Book of Dreams, 2001)*.

- When you're visualizing, when you've got that picture playing out in your mind, always and only dwell upon the end result *(Mike Dooley, The Secret [film])*.

- Art defies defeat by its very existence, representing the celebration of life, in spite of all attempts to degrade and destroy it *(Nadine Gordimer)*.

Positive Thinking / Optimism / Attitude

True Life Story by Angie Milki

I've read several books and listened to countless audios over the years. With a notepad, pen and a highlighter in hand, I am always ready to outline a word, a phrase or a paragraph that resonates with me. I love positive quotes and powerful sayings. And amongst many, one in particular has truly saved my life.

"You get back what you send out"

When we are young, we are told to be different, to be unique in our ways and to separate ourselves from the norm. We begin to think "I'm better" or "I'm number one", when in reality, we are all equally the same. When understanding the concept of oneness, (I am you and you are me) and the law of attraction (you get back what you send out), your mind shifts from an ego mentality to living a life with meaning and on purpose. We begin to see others as we see ourselves and as we strive to be winners, we then want others to win. In fact, giving our energy away to better others will always come back to us, tenfold.

The Universe works in magical ways and is eager to help us in all aspects of life. Most people believe that they must be in control of everything or nothing will get done. I'm sure we've experienced it for ourselves or have certainly met some, if not many people with this mindset. This is a fear-based mindset. Feeling upset, sad, angry, depressed, scared, lonely, etc, these are all emotions that stem from being afraid. When you find yourself experiencing a darker emotion, you must accept and release. Accept and acknowledge your state, then simply release all fears to the Universe. Letting go will free your heart and your mind and will then allow you to move forward with strength. By doing this, you are shifting your mind to a brighter place and this will allow positive experiences to enter your world.

You get back what you send out, that is the law of attraction. That is the beauty of life. We create our own reality and every thought counts. Our subconscious mind does not know what is real and what is not, so feed it thoughts of love and kindness and it will attract those thoughts into your life. This concept has helped me in all areas of my life. When you believe that you do get back what you send out, your outlook on life completely changes. It's quite simple; if you send out negative energy, you will receive negative. If you send out positive energy, you will receive positive. In the way we interact with each other to our own self-talk, it is vital to think, speak and focus on positive, because what you focus on grows.
- Contributed by **Angie Milki**

True Life Story by James Deahl

"Every day can be a good day or a bad day. When I wake up in the morning, I ALWAYS choose to have a good day"
   - ***Jackie Washington*** (November 12, 1919 – June 27, 2009)

I only knew Jackie Washington by reputation until I moved to Hamilton in 1994. It seems to be impossible to live in The Hammer for very long without meeting Jackie. He was everywhere with a guitar and a song. Jackie was the most joyful man I've ever met.

He often said that he was so happy because he always decided to have a good day *every* day regardless of circumstances that no one could alter or work around. He tried to modify the negative things he encountered. But those things beyond human control he merely accepted.

When a family member died, Jackie openly accepted, and lived, that grief. When his many health problems eventually forced him into a nursing home, he accepted that too. Jackie chose not to dwell on, or worry about, past events. No one can go back and re-live a life. He would, as much as possible, live in, and enjoy, the present moment with a song and a smile.

In recent years I have attempted to follow the example set by Jackie Washington. For instance, yesterday a friend discovered two errors in my new poetry book. This book was preceded by nineteen other books and chapbooks, all of which I believe to be error free. Needless to say, I was quite upset from that moment until bedtime. Although the errors still smart, I decided to have a good, enjoyable day when I awoke this morning. The fact is that nothing can change those two mistakes. Nothing. Therefore, there is no point in remaining angry at myself. Turns out that I am human and certainly not perfect. Humbling, to be sure, but not the end of my life.

Prior to my meeting Jackie, I surely would have remained upset for days. Jackie's observation "Why allow something that occurred yesterday ruin today?" has often helped keep me sane. Needless to say, it is not always possible to accept pain, loss, or disappointment. I can but try. – By **James Deahl**

James Deahl was born in Pittsburgh (U.S.A.) in 1945, and grew up in that city as well as in and around the Laurel Highlands Region of the Appalachian Mountains. He moved to Canada in 1970 and holds dual American/Canadian citizenship. He is the author of more than twenty literary titles including:

1. Rooms The Wind Makes (*Guernica Editions Inc.*)
2. North Of Belleville (*Hidden Book Press, 2012*)
3. Opening the Stone Heart (*Aeolus House, 2010*)
4. No Star Is Lost (*Lyricalmyrical, 2009*)

And many more titles ...

James Deahl presently lives in Sarnia and he is the father of Sarah, Simone, and Shona. Address: 985 Maxwell St., Apt. 112, Sarnia, ON N7S 4G2

Quotes on Positive Thinking / Optimism / Attitude

- Although the world is full of suffering, it is full also of the overcoming of it. My optimism, then, does not rest on the absence of evil, but on a glad belief in the preponderance of good and a willing effort always to cooperate with the good, that it may prevail. I try to increase the power God has given me to see the best in everything and everyone, and make that Best a part of my life *(Helen Keller, Optimism, 1903)*.

- Education consists mainly in what we have unlearned *(Mark Twain, Mark Twain's Notebook, 1935, p. 346)*.

- Could we change our attitude, we should not only see life differently, but life itself would come to *be* different. Life would undergo a change of appearance because we ourselves had undergone a change of attitude *(A. R. Orage, "Talks with Katherine*

Mansfield at Fontainebleau," The Century Magazine, November 1924).

- When you are thwarted, it is your own attitude that is out of order (*Meister Eckhart*).

- I always like to look on the optimistic side of life, but I am realistic enough to know that life is a complex matter. With the laugh comes the tears and in developing motion pictures or television shows, you must combine all the facts of life — drama, pathos and humour *(Walt Disney, How to Be Like Walt : Capturing the Magic Every Day of Your Life, 2004, Ch. 1 : It All Started with a Boy, p. 16)*.

- I wouldn't say I'm pessimistic or optimistic. I'm more realistic, I guess. But not cynical. I look. I watch *(Johnny Depp, Anthony Decurtis, "Rolling Stone 30th Anniversary Special: Johnny Depp," Rolling Stone 1998)*.

- Those who have easy, cheerful attitudes tend to be happier than those with less pleasant temperaments, regardless of money, "making it", or success, *(Dr. Joyce Brothers, Wisdom for the Soul: Five Millennia of Prescriptions for Spiritual Healing, 2006 by Larry Chang, p. 71)*.

- There is no such thing as can't, only won't *(Jan Ashford)*.

- Nothing can stop the man with the right mental attitude from achieving his goal *(Thomas Jefferson as quoted in The Greatest Quotations of All-Time by Anthony St Peter, 2010, p. 268)*.

- Everything can be taken from a person but one thing: the last of the human freedoms – the right to choose one's attitude in any given set of circumstances, the right to choose one's way *(Viktor Frankl, Man's Search for Meaning, 2000, p. 75)*.

- If you can't change your fate, change your attitude *(Amy Tan, The Opposite of Fate, 2004)*.

Thought / Mind

- Thoughts mixed with definiteness of purpose, persistence, and burning desires are powerful things *(Napoleon Hill, The Law of Success, 1937)*

- The pearl of the mind is the inner wealth *(Guru Nanak Dev, Guru Granth Sahib, 414-5)*.

- Learn to become still and take your attention away from what you don't want and all the emotional charge around it and place the attention on what you wish to experience *(Rev. Michael Beckwith, The Secret [film])*.

- When thoughts arise, then do all things arise. When thoughts vanish, then do all things vanish *(The Zen Teachings of Huang Po, 1958, p.80)*.

- Those who seek the truth by means of intellect and learning only get further and further away from it. Not 'till your thoughts cease all their branching here and there, not till you abandon all thoughts of seeking for something, not till your mind is motionless as wood or stone, will you be on the right road to the Gate *(The Zen Teachings of Huang Po, 1958, p.79)*.

- Remember that all is opinion *(Marcus Aurelius, Meditations II: 15)*.

- The universe is change; our life is what our thoughts make it *(Marcus Aurelius, Meditations IV: 3)*.

- Do not think that what is hard for you to master is humanly impossible; but if a thing is humanly possible, consider it to be within your reach *(Marcus Aurelius, Meditations VI: 19)*.

- Learning without thought is labour lost and thought without learning is dangerous *(Confucius, Analects 2:15)*. All that is comes from the mind, based on and fashioned by the mind *(Buddha, Dhammapada 1: 1)*.

- The actuality of thought is life

(Aristotle, Metaphysics XII: 7).

- As a man thinketh in his heart, so is he *(Proverbs 23:7)*. Genius is the ability to put into effect what is in your mind *(F. Scott Fitzgerald)*.

- Win the mind; win the world *(Guru Nanak, Guru Granth Sahib 6-17)*.

- There are two things over which you have complete dominion, authority and control – your mind and your mouth *(Molefi Asante as quoted in Acts of Faith, Iyanla Vanzant, 2001, p. 27)*.

- If you don't like the effects of your life, you have to change the nature of your thinking *(Marianne Williamson, A Return to Love, 1992)*.

- If the mind is empty, it is always ready for anything; it is open to everything. In the beginner's mind there are many possibilities, in the expert's mind there are few *(Suzuki, Shunryu, Zen Mind, Beginner's Mind; p. 21)*.

- A reflective, contended mind is the best possession *(Zoroaster, Ushtavaiti Gatha Yasna 43: 15)*.

- One is where one thinks *(Yehuda Ashlag as quoted in Kabbalah for the Student, 2008, p. 193)*.

Wisdom / Insight / Knowledge / Discernment / Judgment

- Don't gain the world and lose your soul, wisdom is better than silver or gold

(Bob Marley, "Zion Train," Uprising, 1980).

- By three methods we may learn wisdom: First, by reflection, which is noblest; Second, by imitation, which is easiest; and third by experience, which is the bitterest *(Confucius).*

- The wise speak of only what they know – Gandalf (J.R.R. Tolkien, The Two Towers, p. 536).

- Say to yourself in the early morning: "I shall meet today inquisitive, ungrateful, violent, treacherous, envious, uncharitable men. All these things have come upon them through ignorance of real good and ill" *(Marcus Aurelius, Meditations II: 1).*

- Medicine heals diseases of the body, wisdom frees the soul from passions *(Democritus quoted in Kathleen Freeman, Ancilla to the Pre-Socratic Philosophers: A Complete Translation, 1948, p. 149).*

- Wisdom lies in stating when you know something and admitting when you do not know

(Confucius, Analects 2: 17).

- You have no idea of the tremendous release and deep peace that comes from meeting yourself and your brother totally without judgement

(A Course in Miracles, 2007, p. 47).

- We judge ourselves by what we feel capable of doing, while others judge us by what we have already done *(Henry Wadsworth Longfellow, Kavanagh: A Tale, 1849)*.

- In case of dissension, never dare to judge till you've heard the other side *(Euripides, Heraclidae)*.

- The feeling of right or wrong is the beginning of wisdom *(Mencius, The Mencius 2A: 6)*.

- The fear of the Lord is the beginning of knowledge: but fools despise wisdom and instruction *(Proverbs 1:7)*.

- For wisdom is better than rubies; and all the things that may be desired are not to be compared to it *(Proverbs 8:11)*.

- The knowledge of anything, since all things have causes, is not acquired or complete unless it is known by its causes *(Avicenna, "On Medicine")*.

- Knowledge, like wealth, is intended for use *(Hermes Trismegistus in The Kybalion: A Study of the Hermetic Philosophy of Ancient Egypt and Greece, 1908)*.

- No tool is more beneficial than intelligence. No enemy is more harmful than ignorance *(Al-Shaykh Al-Mufid)*.

- You want weapons? We're in a library! Books! The best weapons in the world *(Doctor Who)*.

- The great end of learning is nothing else but to seek for the lost mind *(Mencius, Works VI, I: 11.4)*.

FIRE

The qualities of this chapter are focused on Fire, where you get in touch with your emotions, devotion, and love. You experience illumination, enlightenment, clarification, purification, Self-growth, and learn to live from a consciousness of Self/Ego-Transcendence. You intone "I Love" based on your experience of emotional awareness, and Self/Ego-Transcendence, with a heightened sense of compassion. As you read the quotes related to the element Fire, get in touch with the compassionate qualities highlighted in various topics and true life stories throughout this chapter.

The Fire domain asks that we begin with Self love, yet transcend our Ego and self-absorbed desires. Ego then becomes sublimated in service of a higher cause, and in harmony with Divine Will. Reconnect with devotion, love, selflessness and compassion. *Jimi Hendrix* captures the principle of heart-centered living in the following quote:

"When the power of love overcomes the love of power the world will know peace"

True Life Story / Roeland Peter Hommerson

I am retired now for seven years. A person that I have been inspired by is Dr. Michael Mallot, who gave me his own quote which I have remembered for years ...

"You are only ever as happy as your least happy child"
- Dr. Michael Mallot

When something inspires me in life I like to set it to words. I wrote the following poem while in Elliot Lake, 2009:

...lost in the moment,
Without time or space,
Deep in the memory caverns of my mind,
An almost forgotten place,

Where time has no clock,
And distance no measure.
There ... often solace I find ...
And subdued treasure ...
Sadness and joy are what lay in store,
And I shall place them carefully
On memory's shore.

While writing the above poem I was pondering life. My wife had passed away, and I was beset with family challenges.

I was left with two teenage children, which was the beginning of my journey as a single parent. I was thinking about the past.

Sometimes all you have are memories ... there is no right or wrong with grieving, everyone has their own individual experience, everyone is different; you will never really get over the loss of a spouse and you do not have to get over it ... just cherish the memories ...

Contributed by **Roeland Peter Hommersen,** Hamilton, Ontario, Canada petehommerson@gmail.com

Emotional Quotes

Emotions are one of the most powerful forces in human life. When you feel love, compassion ... empathy and service well up in your heart, you feel alive.

"I Love"

Relational

Compassion / Kindness / Empathy / Sympathy / Charity

True Life Story by Yuwaraj Singh Jina

"Your truest character is most accurately measured by how you treat those who can do 'NOTHING' for you … ! It is very simple and true …!"
- **Yuwaraj Singh Jina**

Most of the time, this holds on, if you don't have any compulsions, distractions, obligations … when you can REALLY give something to someone, who will never be in a position to repay or give you back! At times … it looks very inappropriate, … but I prefer to think it is –
Radical Honesty… !! and in fact what screws us up most in life … is the picture in our head of how it is supposed to be…

We start expecting endlessly, and there, we fail.
Wisdom & 'Good Thoughts', should not be only said in 'WORDS' but converted into 'ACTION', then only one can feel privileged, esteemed and closer to one's own SOUL … !!
- Contributed by **Yuwaraj Singh Jina**
  Jalandhar, India
  (studied at Glancy Medical College, Amritsar)

Quotes: Compassion/Kindness/ Empathy/sympathy

- Remember that the people you are talking to are a hundred times more interested in themselves and their wants and problems than they are in you and your problems *(Dale Carnegie)*.

- This virtue, one of the noblest with which man is endowed, seems to arise incidentally from our sympathies becoming more tender and more widely diffused, until they are extended to all sentient beings *(Charles Darwin, The Descent of Man, 1871)*.

- Whenever you feel like criticizing any one... just remember that all the people in this world haven't had the advantages that you've had *(F. Scott Fitzgerald, The Great Gatsby, 1925)*.

- It's very easy to feel someone's pain when you love them *(Salma Hayek, "Conversation with Salma Hayek," 2002)*.

- Sometimes I enter prayer and I intend to prolong it, but then I hear a child crying, and I shorten my prayer thinking of the distress of the child's mother *(Prophet Muhammad, Fiqh us-Sunnah, Vol. 2, Number 51b)*.

- Where there is charity and wisdom, there is neither fear nor ignorance *(St. Francis of Assisi, The Counsels of the Holy Father St. Francis, Admonition 27)*.

- While we do our good works let us not forget that the real solution lies in a world in which charity will have become unnecessary *(Chinua Achebe, Anthills of the Savannah, 2012)*.

- No act of kindness, no matter how small, is ever wasted *(Aesop, The Lion and the Mouse)*.

- People will forget what you said
  People will forget what you did
  But people will never forget how you made them feel *(Maya Angelou, Worth Repeating: More Than 5,000 Classic and Contemporary Quotes, 2003 by Bob Kelly, p. 263)*.

- If you want others to be happy, practice compassion. If you want to be happy, practice compassion *(Meditations for Living In Balance: Daily Solutions for People Who Do Too Much, 2000 by Anne Wilson Schaef, p. 11)*.

Compassion and tolerance are not a sign of weakness, but a sign of strength *(Dalai Lama, Words Of Wisdom: Selected Quotes by His Holiness the Dalai Lama, 2001 edited by Margaret Gee, p. 71)*.

Wise Words

- You may call God love, you may call God goodness. But the best name for God is compassion *(Meister Eckhart)*.

- We should be kind and compassionate with those who are sad or tempted, speak at length with them, and show great joy and cheerfulness, both interior and exterior, to draw them to the opposite of what they feel, for their greater edification and consolation *(St. Ignatius of Loyola, "On Dealing with Others," Rome, early September 1541)*.

- These problems do not disappear just because we do not hear about them. There is so much more happening around the world than what is communicated to us about the top stories we do hear. We all need to look deeper and discover for ourselves.... What is the problem? Where is it? How can we help to solve it? *(Angelina Jolie, Notes from My Travels: Visits with Refugees in Africa, Cambodia, Pakistan and Ecuador, 2006)*.

- If a man shuts his ears to the cry of the poor, he too will cry out and not be answered *(Proverbs 21:13)*.

- Do not withhold good from those who deserve it, when it is in your power to act *(Proverbs 3:27)*.

- For I desire mercy, and not sacrifice, and the knowledge of God rather than burnt-offerings *(Hosea 6:6)*.

- Find and follow the good path and be ruled by compassion. For if the various ways are examined, compassion will prove the means to liberation *(Thiruvalluvar, Tirukkural 25: 241-242)*.

- In dealing with others, be gentle and kind *(Lao Tzu, Tao Te Ching 8)*.

- To use bitter words, when kind words are at hand, Is like picking unripe fruit when the ripe fruit is there *(Thiruvalluvar, Tirukkural Verse X.10)*.

- If we could read the secret history of our enemies, we should find in each man's life sorrow and suffering enough to disarm all hostility *(Henry Wadsworth Longfellow, Driftwood, 1857)*.

- The feeling of consideration is the beginning of humanity *(Mencius, The Mencius 2A: 6)*.

- Love the sinner and hate the sin *(St. Augustine, Opera Omnia, II, 962: 211)*.

- You know, you can steel your heart against any kind of trouble, any kind of horror. But the simple act of kindness from a complete stranger will unstitch you *(Chris Abani)*.

- The Mercy of Allah is an Ocean, Our sins are a lump of clay clenched between the beak of a pigeon. The pigeon is perched on the branch of a tree at the edge of that ocean. It only has to open its beak

(Leila Aboulela, Minaret, 2006, p. 4).

- The whole idea of compassion, which is central to Mahayana Buddhism, is based on a keen awareness of the interdependence of all these living beings, which are all part of one another, and all involved in one another *(Thomas Merton, The Asian Journal of Thomas Merton, 1975, p. 341)*.

- Compassion is the basis of all truthful relationships: it means being present with love – for ourselves and for all life, including animals, fish, birds, and trees *(Ram Dass, Setting Out on the Path of Service, 1992)*.

- When we finally know we are dying, and all other sentient beings are dying with us, we start to have a burning, almost heartbreaking sense of fragility and preciousness of each moment and each Being, and from this can grow a deep, clear, limitless compassion for all beings *(Sogyal Rinpoche, The Tibetan Book of Living and Dying, 1994, p. 191)*.

Co-Creation / Co-operation / Connectedness / Interdependence

- I'm confident that there is a bigger force at work with all of us, and that if you are willing to submit yourself, to allow yourself to align with whatever that is, whatever that dream or vision is for yourself, then you can do great things in your life *(Oprah Winfrey, Larry King Live Interview, 4 September 2001)*.

- Try your best and let the universe do the rest *(Harbhajan Singh Yogi)*.

- Today we must abandon competition and secure cooperation. This must be the central fact in all our considerations of international affairs; otherwise we face certain disaster *(Albert Einstein, Only Then Shall We Find Courage, 1946)*.

- This dew-like life fades away; time speeds swiftly. In this short life of ours, avoid involvement in superfluous things and just study the Way *(Shobogenzo Zuimonki, 1975, Dogen 5:8)*.

- Interdependence is and ought to be as much the ideal of man as self-sufficiency. Man is a social being. Without interrelation with society he cannot realize his oneness with the universe and suppress his egotism *(Mahatma Gandhi as quoted in Beyond the American Dream by Charles D. Hayes, 1998, p. 184)*.

- Synergy means that the whole is greater than the sum of its parts *(Stephen Covey, The 7 Habits of Highly Effective People, 2004, p. 117)*.

- In critical moments even the very powerful have need of the weakest *(Aesop, The Lion and the Mouse)*.

- Win/Win is based on the paradigm that there is plenty for everybody, that one person's success is not achieved at the expense of exclusion of the success of others. *(Stephen Covey, The 7 Habits of Highly Effective People, 1989)*.

- What is required is a new mindset and a change of heart, to be able to see the person across the ocean as our neighbour *(Mohamed ElBaradei, Nobel lecture, 2005)*.

- When we survey our lives and endeavours we soon observe that almost the whole of our actions and desires are bound up with the existence of other human beings *(Albert Einstein, The World As I See It, 1949)*.

- People will always reach over the impenetrable roar of political discourse to help a human on the other side *(Sir Bob Geldof commenting on Band Aid and Live Aid)*.

- We can no longer afford indifference to suffering outside our borders; nor can we consume the world's resources without regard to effect. For the world has changed, and we must change with it *(Barack Obama, Inaugural Address, 2009)*.

Devotion / Sincerity

- I do not pray for success, I ask for faithfulness *(Mother Theresa)*.

- Serve the LORD thy God with all your heart and with all your soul *(Deuteronomy 10:12)*.

- Even kings and emperors, with mountains of property and oceans of wealth are not even equal to an ant, who does not forget God *(Guru Nanak Dev, Guru Granth Sahib, 5-6)*.

- The supreme Lord who pervades all existence, the true Self of all creatures, may be realized through undivided love *(Bhagavad Gita 8:22)*.

- Faithless is he that says farewell when the road darkens – Gandalf *(J.R.R. Tolkien, The Fellowship of the Ring, 367)*.

- Hold faithfulness and sincerity as first principles *(Confucius, Analects 1: 8, ii)*.

- You shall love the Lord your God with all your heart, all your soul, and with all your might. These words that I command you today shall be in your heart *(Deuteronomy 6: 5-6)*.

- Favour is deceitful, and beauty is vain, but a woman that feareth the LORD, she shall be praised *(Proverbs 31:30)*.

- You have made us for yourself, O Lord, and our hearts are restless until they rest in you *(St. Augustine, Confessions 1: 1)*.

- True piety does not consist in turning your faces to the east or the west *(Quran, Surah 2:177)*.

- We created man and know the promptings of his heart, being nearer to him than his jugular vein *(Quran 50:16)*.

Emotions / Feelings

- Emotional life is a domain that, as surely as math or reading, can be handled with greater or lesser skill, and requires its unique set of competencies. And how adept a person is at those is crucial to understanding why one person thrives in life while another, of equal intellect, dead-ends: emotional aptitude is a meta-ability, determining how well we can use whatever other skills we have, including raw intellect *(Daniel Goleman, Emotional Intelligence: Why It Can Matter More Than IQ, 1995).*

- Every emotion, from despair all of the way up to ecstasy; from complete Connection to who-you-really-are, all the way to pinching yourself off pretty severely, all of those emotions are about your perception of freedom, or your perception of bondage—every one of them *(Abraham-Hicks).*

- Emotion is the chief source of all becoming-conscious. There can be no transforming of darkness into light and of apathy into movement without emotion *(Carl Jung, Psychological Aspects of the Modern Archetype, 1938).*

- We should not pretend to understand the world only by the intellect; we apprehend it just as much by feeling *(Carl Jung).*

- God turns you from one feeling to another and teaches by means of opposites, so that you will have two wings to fly, not one *(Rumi, The Paradoxes of Love by Llewellyn Vaughan-Lee, 1996, p. 96).*

- If we try to get rid of negative feelings, we don't realize that those feelings are our wisdom *(Pema Chödrön, Start Where You Are, 1994).*

Forgiveness

- Father, forgive them; for they know not what they do *(Jesus Christ, Luke 23:34, uttered from the cross, asking forgiveness for those who put him to death).*

- Forgiveness is the needle that knows how to mend *(Jewel Kilcher from "Under the Water").*

- The more anger towards the past you carry in your heart, the less capable you are of loving in the present *(Barbara De Angelis)*.

- The weak can never forgive. Forgiveness is the attribute of the strong *(Mahatma Gandhi, Young India, 2 April 1931)*.

- Those who spend freely, whether in prosperity or in adversity, restrain anger and pardon all, please Allah with their good deeds *(Quran 3:134)*.

- The weak can never forgive. Forgiveness is the attribute of the strong *(Mahatma Gandhi)*.

- Forgiveness is the healing of the perception of separation *(A Course in Miracles, 2007, p. 46)*.

- Forgiveness is an absolute necessity for continued human existence *(Desmond Tutu quoted in Beyond Anger by Larry Yeagley, 2006, p. 108)*.

- Without forgiveness there can be no future for a relationship between individuals or within and between nations *(Desmond Tutu, "Truth and Reconciliation," BBC Focus on Africa, January-March 2000)*.

- Anger is like holding onto a red hot coal with the intent to throw it at somebody else. But you are the one who gets burned *(Buddha)*.

- To err is human, to forgive Divine *(Alexander Pope, An Essay on Criticism, 1711)*.

- It is in pardoning that we are pardoned *(St Francis of Assisi)*.

- We cannot love unless we have accepted forgiveness, and the deeper our experience of forgiveness is, the greater is our love *(Paul Tillich, The New Being, 2005, p. 10)*.

- Oh Farid, do not strike back those who hit you with their fists *(Baba Farid)*.

Friendship

True Life Story by Emily Mumma

"Good friends are like stars...
You don't always see them,
But you know they are always there" Anonymous

This quote was sent to me by a relatively new friend who resides as a winter resident in the community of 55 plus where I live year round. I first learned to know Richard as we served together on the Board of Directors for this community. Our respect for one another, the creative thinking we prompted in one another – especially when we held differing views – was the beginning of what grew into an interesting friendship.

Sometimes friendship depends on frequency of seeing and being with one another. Other times that is less important. Friendship is a multi-faceted experience – in many ways like a diamond held in the light – offering a rainbow of many colours.

I enjoy people whose personality opens opportunities to see life differently, to think outside the box, yet at the same time affirm who I am and who are willing to accept what I have to offer ... a kind of mutuality.

Perhaps all of that is to say, friendship includes someone who is easy to be around; someone who invites me to be me and expects from me that same kind of freedom to be her/him self.

No walking on eggshells or ice. The kind of relationship which embraces deep thinking and which delights equally in humour and fun.

Friendship is nearly impossible to define, but can be described and felt when words fail. One knows intuitively the level of friendship one prefers.

Yes, I believe there are many kinds of friendship ... each fulfilling a specific need in another person's life. Consequently, I have many people I claim as "friend".

As I approach nearly 80 years on this Earth, I am awed by the number of friends from such varied backgrounds and life experiences, most living in various places across the U.S. and elsewhere.

There are times I'm troubled because I have neither the energy or time to be connected as I'd prefer. Then the quote above comforts my spirit.

Also, I find comfort in memories of times we were together, laughed, wept, puzzled, reflected, prayed, sang, played, sat in silence, ate, struggled, pondered, waited, and sometimes said our Earthly "good-byes".

Those memories are tied into these two parting quotes:

"People don't care how much you know
Until they know how much you care."
- Seen in Guideposts Magazine Jan. 2008

"People will forget what you said; they will forget what you did.

People will never forget how you made them feel."
- Rec'd in an e-mail from a friend in 2005

Contributed by **Emily Mumma**
Lorida, Florida, U.S.A.

Quotes on Friendship

I was angry with my friend:
I told my wrath, my wrath did end.
I was angry with my foe:I told it not, my wrath did grow *(William Blake, A Poison Tree, stanza 1).*

Wise Words

A single rose can be my garden... a single friend, my world *(Leo Buscaglia)*.

- Things are never quite as scary when you've got a best friend *(Calvin, The Indispensable Calvin and Hobbes p77)*.

- Misfortune shows those who are not really friends *(Aristotle, Eudemian Ethics VII.1238a20)*.

- Nor can goodness and evil be equal. Repel evil with what is better: Then will hatred between you and another turn to close friendship. *(Quran41:34)*

- As the quality of water changes with the nature of the soil; So will a man's reason vary with the quality of his friends *(Tiruvalluvar, Tirukkural Verse XLVI.2)*.

- It is useless to meet revenge with revenge: it will heal nothing – Frodo *(J.R.R. Tolkien, The Return of the King, p. 1056)*.

- I always felt that the great high privilege, relief and comfort of friendship was that one had to explain nothing *(Katherine Mansfield quoted in Katherine Mansfield: A Biography, 1953 by Anto Alpers, p. 266)*.

- Misfortune shows those who are not really friends *(Aristotle, Eudemian Ethics VII. 1238a20)*.

- Friends share all things *(Pythagoras as quoted in Diongenes Laertius, Lives of Eminent Philosophers VIII: 10)*.

- Of all the means which wisdom acquires to ensure happiness throughout the whole of life, by far the most important is friendship. *(Epicurus, Sovereign Maxims 28)*.

- Friendship makes prosperity more shining and lessens adversity by dividing and sharing it *(Cicero, De Amicitia)*.
- With a thousand friends you have not a friend to spare, but a single enemy you will meet everywhere *(Imam Ali)*.

- A friend cannot be considered a true friend unless tested on three occasions: in time of need, behind your back, and after your death *(Imam Ali, Nahj ul-Balāgha)*.

Asking / Giving / Receiving

- If you knew what I know about the power of giving, you would not let a single meal pass without sharing it in some way *(Buddha)*.

- If you're in the luckiest 1 per cent of humanity, you owe it to the rest of humanity to think about the other 99 per cent *(Warren Buffet, Times Online, 28 June, 2007)*.

- The gifts of caring, attention, affection, appreciation, and love are some of the most precious gifts you can give, and they don't cost you anything *(Deepak Chopra, The Seven Spiritual Laws of Success, 1994)*.

- It is well to give when asked, but it is better to give unasked, through understanding *(Kahlil Gibran)*. You give before you get *(Napoleon Hill, The Law of Success, 1937)*.

- The Altruist symbolizes giving and abundance, but only that type of giving about which you are passionate, not what you think the world expects from you *(From Carol S. Pearson, The Hero Within)*.

- The Lord can give, and the Lord can take away. I might be herding sheep next year *(Elvis Presley)*.

Ability is nothing without opportunity *(Napoléon Bonaparte)*.

- We are Divine enough to ask and we are important enough to receive *(Wayne Dyer)*.

- Be generous but not extravagant; be frugal but not miserly *(Imam Ali)*.

- Sell your possessions and give to the poor. Provide purses for yourselves that will not wear out, a treasure in heaven that will not be exhausted, where no thief comes near and no moth destroys *(Luke 12:33)*.

- Command those who are rich in this present world not to be arrogant nor to put their hope in wealth, which is so uncertain, but to put their hope in God, who richly provides us with everything for our enjoyment. Command them to do good, to be rich in good deeds, and to be generous and willing to share. In this way they will lay up treasure for themselves as a firm foundation for the coming age, so that they may take hold of the life that is truly life *(1 Timothy 6: 17-19)*.

- You shall give the appropriate charity to the relatives, the needy, the poor, and the traveling foreigner, but do not be excessive or extravagant *(Quran 17:26)*.

- If you disclose acts of charity, even so it is well but if you conceal them and make them reach those really in need, that is best for you *(Quran 2:271)*.

- Having, First, gained all you can, and, Secondly saved all you can, Then give all you can *(John Wesley, Sermon 50 "The Use of Money" in The Works of the Reverend John Wesley, A.M., 1840 edited by John Emory, Vol. I, p. 446)*.

Heart

- Nothing brings joy as does a tamed, controlled, attended and restrained heart. This heart brings joy *(Buddha, Anguttara Nikaya)*.

- In life to handle yourself, use your head, but to handle others, use your heart *(Chinmayananda)*.

- There is a wisdom of the Head, and ... there is a wisdom of the Heart *(Charles Dickens, Hard Times, 1854, Bk. III, Ch. 1)*.

- There is a road in the hearts of all of us, hidden and seldom traveled, which leads to an unknown, secret place *(Luther Standing Bear)*.

Humility

- Just because I managed to do a little something, I don't want anyone back home to think I got a big head *(Elvis Presley)*.

- Such is oft the course of deeds that move the wheels of the world: small hands do them because they must, while the eyes of the great are elsewhere – Elrond *(J.R.R. Tolkien, The Fellowship of the Ring, 367)*.

- As for me, all I know is that I know nothing *(Socrates as quoted in Republic by Plato, 354b)*.

- Humility, a sense of reverence before the sons of heaven — of all the prizes that a mortal man might win, these, I say, are wisest; these are best *(Euripides, Bacchae 1: 1150)*.

- Sweetness of speech and humility are the essence of virtues *(Guru Nanak, Guru Granth Sahib 470:13)*.

- Successful indeed are the believers, those who humble themselves in their prayers *(Quran 23:1-2)*.

- In the realm of humility, the Word is Beauty *(Guru Nanak, Guru Granth Sahib, p.8)*.

- True humility is strength, not weakness. It disarms antagonism and ultimately conquers it (Meher Baba, Life at Its Best, 1957, 25-26).

- "Ego does not come with love. Ego walks alone, and love walks in oneness."

   - Satish Kaku, Bombay, India (original quote)

- The greater your capacity to love, the greater your capacity to feel the pain *(Jennifer Aniston, Oprah Magazine, 2004).*

Say you don't need no diamond ring and I'll be satisfied
Tell me that you want the kind of thing that money just can't buy
I don't care too much for money, money can't buy me love *(The Beatles, "Can't Buy Me Love").*

- All you need is love, love. Love is all you need *(The Beatles, Magical Mystery Tour, 1967, "All You Need Is Love").*

- A girl in a convertible is worth five in the phonebook *(Berkshire Hathaway 2000 Chairman's Letter).*

- It is when we ask for love less and begin giving it more that the basis of human love is revealed to us *(Leo Buscaglia, Born For Love, 1994).*

- Don't hold to anger, hurt or pain. They steal your energy and keep you from *love (Leo Buscaglia).*

- I have a very strong feeling that the opposite of love is not hate - it's apathy. It's not giving a damn *(Leo Buscaglia).*

- It is difficult for some people to accept that love is a choice. This seems to run counter to the generally accepted theory of romantic love which expounds that love is inborn and as such requires no more than to accept it *(Leo Buscaglia).*

- One does not fall "in" or "out" of love. One grows in love. *(Leo Buscaglia, LOVE, 1972)*

- Love is the greatest persuasive power we know in life *(Chinmayananda).*

- You can't be wise and in love at the same time *(Bob Dylan, No Direction Home, 2005).*

- Love is the ultimate and the highest goal to which man can aspire *(Viktor Frankl, Man's Search For Meaning, 1946).*

- Selfish persons are incapable of loving others, but they are not capable of loving themselves either *(Erich Fromm, Man for Himself, 1947, Ch. 4).*

- Immature love says: "I love you because I need you." Mature love says: "I need you because I love you" *(Erich Fromm, The Art of Loving, Ch. 2).*

- Love possesses not nor would it be possessed; For love is sufficient unto love *(Kahlil Gibran, The Prophet, 1923).*

- When the power of love overcomes the love of power the world will know peace *(Jimi Hendrix).*

- Above all do not forget your duty to love yourself *(Søren Kierkegaard, Letter to Hans Peter, his cousin, 1848).*

- Darkness cannot drive out darkness: only light can do that. Hate cannot drive out hate: only love can do that *(Martin Luther King Jr., Strength to Love, 1963, Ch. 5: Loving your enemies).*

- To love at all is to be vulnerable. Love anything, and your heart will certainly be wrung and possibly be broken *(C.S. Lewis, The Four Loves, 1960).*

- The more you are motivated by love, the more fearless and free your actions will be *(Katherine Mansfield).*

- And in the end, the love you take is equal to the love you make *(Beatles, "The End"; The last full song track of Abbey Road, 1969).*
- We created man and know the promptings of his heart, being nearer to him than his jugular vein *(Quran 50:16).*

- In one kiss, you'll know all I haven't said *(Pablo Neruda, Twenty Love Poems and a Song of Despair, 1924, XIV, trans. William Merwin, Penguin Classics, 1993, p. 37).*

- Grief is the price we pay for love *(Queen Elizabeth II, in a letter read at the memorial for British victims of the 9/11 attacks held in New York).*

- The salvation of man is through love and in love. I understood how a man who has nothing left in this world still may know bliss, be it only for a brief moment, in the contemplation of his beloved *(Viktor Frankl, Man's Search For Meaning, 1946).*

- Faced with today's problems and disappointments, many people will try to escape from their responsibility. Escape in selfishness, escape in sexual pleasure, escape in drugs, escape in violence, escape in indifference and cynical attitudes. I propose to you the option of love, which is the opposite of escape *(Pope John Paul II, Said during his first visit to the US in 1979).*

- Love comes when manipulation stops; when you think more about the other person than about his or her reactions to you. When you dare to reveal yourself fully. When you dare to be vulnerable *(Dr. Joyce Brothers, Courage: The Choice That Makes the Difference, 2004 by Dwight GoldWinde, p. 93).*

- Teach only love for that is what you are (*A Course in Miracles*, 2007, p. 99).

- Love is an energy which exists of itself. It is its own value *(Thornton Wilder, TIME magazine, 3 February 1958)*.

- Love is all we have, the only way that each can help the other *(Euripides – Orestes I. 298)*.

- Love conquers all things; let us too surrender to love *(Virgil, Eclogues X: 69)*.

- So I can't live either without you or with you *(Ovid, Amores III, xi: 39)*.

- If you want to be loved, be lovable *(Ovid, Ars Amatoria II: 107)*.

- The heart unites whatever the mind separates, pushes on beyond the arena of necessity and transmutes the struggle into love (Nikos Kazantzakis, *The Saviours of God*, 1923).

- This was love: a string of coincidences that gathered significance and became miracles *(Chimamanda Ngozi Adichie, Half of a Yellow Sun, 2007, 135)*.

- Hearts united in pain and sorrow will not be separated by joy and happiness. Bonds that are woven in sadness are stronger than the ties of joy and pleasure. Love that is washed by tears will remain eternally pure and faithful *(Khalil Gibran, Love Letters in the Sand, 2006)*.

- There is nothing love cannot face; there is no limit to its faith, its hope and its endurance *(I Corinthians 13:7)*.

- The consciousness of loving and being loved brings a warmth and richness to life that nothing else can bring *(Oscar Wilde, Epigrams of Oscar Wilde, 2007, p. 103)*.

- When love revealed its mystery to me, the parroted words vanished. Inside and outside, I was cleansed. I saw my Beloved wherever I looked *(Bulleh Shah)*.

Marriage / Family / Stages of Development

- If you get bored with the person you married for love, there's something wrong with you - not with that person *(Shahrukh Khan)*.

- If we want to pass on high expectations to our children, we have to have higher expectations for ourselves *(Barack Obama, The Audacity of Hope, 2006, p.347)*.

- Having a child changes every aspect of your life — for the better, of course. The sacrifices are large, but what you get in return is even bigger than the sacrifices you make. I feel, in a sense, ready to die because you are living on in your *child (November 2007 interview remarks quoted by Susan Chenery, "Who Is That Man?" In Touch Weekly, January 23, 2008)*.

- Having a child changes every aspect of your life — for the better, of course. The sacrifices are large, but what you get in return is even bigger than the sacrifices you make. I feel, in a sense, ready to die because you are living on in your child *(Heath Ledger, November 2007 interview remarks quoted by Susan Chenery, "Who Is That Man?" In Touch Weekly, January 23, 2008)*.

- I now spend a good part of my day dreaming of times past, present and future. As I try to survive on 15 hours sleep a day, I have plenty of time to enjoy vivid dreams. Being completely wheelchaired doesn't stop my mind from roaming the universe — on the contrary! *(Arthur C. Clarke, 90th Birthday Reflections, 2007)*.

- The man who views the world at 50 the same as he did at 20 has wasted 30 years of his life *(Muhammad Ali)*.

- Therefore shall a man leave his father and his mother, and shall cleave unto his wife, and they shall be one flesh *(Genesis 2:24)*.

- As the family goes, so goes the nation and so goes the whole world in which we live (Pope John Paul II).

- The secret of the fountain of youth is to think youthful thoughts *(Josephine Baker quoted in Wisdom for the Soul by Larry Chang, 2006, p. 46)*.

- Marriage is not just spiritual communion and passionate embraces; marriage is also three meals a day, sharing the workload and remembering to carry out the *trash (Dr. Joyce Brothers, "When Your Husband's Affection Cools" in Good Housekeeping, May 1972)*.

- Religious belief, trust, a sense of connection to the universe — no matter what you call it, there is a spiritual component to strong families. They see their lives as imbued with purpose, reflected in the things they do for one another and the community. Small problems provide a chance to grow; large ones are a lesson in courage *(Dr. Joyce Brothers, 10 Keys to a Strong Family, 2002)*.

- Honour your father and your mother, as Jehovah your God has commanded you, so that your days may be prolonged, and so that it may be well in the land which your God is giving to you *(Deuteronomy 5: 16)*.

- And in the end it's not the years in your life that count. It is life in your years *(Abraham Lincoln as quoted in Quotes Junkie Presidents Edition by Hagopian Institute, 2008, p. 4)*.

- You don't choose your family. They are God's gift to you, as you are to them *(Desmond Tutu, Address at Enthronement as Archbishop, 7 September 1986)*.

- The more sand has escaped from the hourglass of our life, the clearer we should see through it *(Johann Richter quoted in Wisdom for the Soul by Larry Chang, 2006, p. 44)*.

- A good marriage is one which allows for change and growth in the individuals and in the way they express their love *(Pearl S. Buck, To My Daughters, With Love, 1967)*.

Non-Violence

- I have consistently preached that nonviolence demands that the means we use must be as pure as the ends we seek *(Martin Luther King Jr., Letter from a Birmingham Jail, 1963)*.

- Nonviolence is the answer to the crucial political and moral questions of our time — the need for mankind to overcome oppression and violence without resorting to violence and oppression *(Martin Luther King, Jr., Nobel Prize acceptance speech, 1964)*.

- This call for a worldwide fellowship that lifts neighbourly concern beyond one's tribe, race, class, and nation is in reality a call for an all-embracing and unconditional love for all mankind *(Martin Luther King, Jr., Beyond Vietnam, 1967)*.

- Respect for all living beings is non-violence *(Mahavira)*.

- Non-violence and kindness to living beings is kindness to oneself *(Mahavira)*.

Passion / Anger / Hate

- To make love a prisoner of the mundane is to take its passion and lose it forever *(Leo Buscaglia).*

- There are things that must evoke our anger to show we care. It is what we do with that anger. If we direct that energy we can use it positively or destructively *(Archbishop Desmond Tutu, Daily Express, 29th October 2008).*

- There is no end. There is no beginning. There is only the infinite passion of life *(Federico Fellini, Fellini on Fellini, 1976 edited by Anna Keel and Christian Strich; translated by Isabel Quigly).*

- If you don't find a way to express your anger, in a direct, constructive way, it will leak out as indirect, covert hostility, or it will eventually burst forth as explosive rage or violence *(Shakti Gawain, Return to the Garden: A Journey of Discovery, 1989).*

- Nothing great in the World has been accomplished without passion *(Hegel, Lectures on the Philosophy of History, 1832).*

Prayer

Lord, make me an instrument of Thy peace. Where there is hatred, let me sow love;
Where there is injury, pardon;

Where there is doubt, faith;
Where there is despair, hope;
Where there is darkness, light;
Where there is sadness, joy.
O Divine Master,
Grant that I may not so much seek
To be consoled as to console,
To be understood as to understand,

To be loved, as to love;
For it is in giving that we receive;
It is in pardoning that we are pardoned;
It is in dying to self that we are born to Eternal Life.
Amen *(St. Francis of Assisi)*.

- We have confused God with Santa Claus. And we believe that prayer means making a list of everything you don't have but want and trying to persuade God you deserve it. Now I'm sorry, that's not God, that's Santa Claus *(Harold Kushner)*.

- The first to be summoned to Paradise on the Day of Resurrection will be those who praise God in prosperity and adversity *(Prophet Muhammad, Al-Tirmidhi, Hadith 730)*.

- I do not pray for success, I ask for faithfulness *(Mother Theresa)*.

- If the only prayer you ever say in your entire life is thank you, it will be enough *(Meister Eckhart)*.

- Calvin: [I pray for] The strength to change what I can, the inability to accept what I can't, and the incapacity to tell the difference *(The Days are Just Packed p. 137)*.

- When thou prayest, enter into thy closet, and when thou hast shut thy door, pray to thy Father in secret; and thy Father shall reward thee openly *(Matthew 6:6)*.

Purification

- The Divine assails the human soul in order to renew it and thus to make it Divine... The soul feels itself to be perishing and melting away. The sensual part is purified in aridity, the faculties are purified in the emptiness of their perceptions and the spirit is purified in thick darkness *(St. John of the Cross, The Dark Night of the Soul, Bk. 2, Ch. 6)*.

- As the soul becomes purged and purified by means of this fire of love, it becomes ever more enkindled in love *(St. John of the Cross, The Dark Night of the Soul, Bk. 2, Ch. 10, #4).*

- Truth is high but higher still is Truthful Living *(Guru Nanak, Guru Granth Sahib, 621).*

- By rituals purity is not obtained even by performance millions of rites *(Guru Nanak, Guru Granth Sahib, 1-5).*

- The enlightened person is blessed with Name, Charity and Purification *(Guru Nanak Dev, 942-4).*

- They are forever free who renounce all selfish desires and break away from the ego-cage of "I," "me," and "mine" to be united with the Lord. Attain to this, and pass from death to immortality *(Bhagavad Gita 2:71).*

- Prosperity is not for the envious, nor is greatness for those of impure conduct *(Thiruvalluvar, Tirukkural 14: 135).*

- One who restrains his anger when it has arisen, as doctors by medicines restrain poison of the snake spreading in the body, that monk leaves this and the further shore, as a snake quits its old worn out skin *(Buddha, Sutta Nipata I.1).*

- The soul that is attached to anything, however much good there may be in it, will not arrive at the liberty of the divine *(St. John of the Cross as quoted in A Path With Heart in Jack Kornfield, 1993, p. 148).*

Relationships / Community

- It's a strange thing that every human being has a sort of dignity or wholeness in him, and out of that develops relationships to other human beings, tensions, misunderstandings, tenderness, coming in contact, touching and being touched, the cutting off of a contact and what happens *then (Ingmar Bergman, Ingmar Bergman Directs, 1972 by John Simon)*.

- All actual life is encounter *(Martin Buber, I And Thou, 1923)*.

- The intelligence of the universe is social *(Marcus Aurelius, Meditations V: 30)*.

Responsibility

- The message has always been the same: that you are responsible for your life *(Oprah Winfrey, "It Is Constant Work," Newsweek, January 2001)*.

- One's philosophy is not best expressed in words; it is expressed in the choices one makes.... In the long run, we shape our lives and we shape ourselves. The process never ends until we die. And, the choices we make are ultimately our own responsibility *(Eleanor Roosevelt, You Learn By Living, Foreword, 1960)*.

- Whatever happens, take responsibility *(Anthony Robbins)*. Freedom and power bring responsibility *(Jawaharlal Nehru, A Tryst With Destiny, 1947)*.

- A man who becomes conscious of the responsibility he bears toward a human being who affectionately waits for him, or to an unfinished work, will never be able to throw away his life. He knows the "why" for his existence, and will be able to bear almost any "how" *(Viktor Frankl, Man's Search For Meaning, 60th anniversary edition, p. 16-17)*.

- Parents can only give good advice or put them on the right paths, but the final forming of a person's character lies in their own hands *(Anne Frank)*.

Service / Altruism / Healing

- The root of happiness is altruism — the wish to be of service to others *(Dalai Lama, The Dalai Lama at Harvard: Lectures on the Buddhist Path to Peace, 1988 by Jeffrey Hopkins)*.

- It is high time the ideal of success should be replaced with the ideal of service ... Only a life lived for others is a life worthwhile *(Albert Einstein, From Wisdom for the Soul: Five Millennia of Prescriptions for Spiritual Healing, 2006 by Larry Chang, p. 330)*.

- Dedicate the precious days of your lives to the betterment of the world *(Bahá'u'lláh)*.

- I will use treatment to help the sick according to my ability and judgment but with never a view to injury and wrongdoing *(Hippocrates – The Hippocratic Oath)*.

- With purity and holiness, I will pass my life and practice the art of medicine *(Hippocrates – The Hippocratic Oath)*.

- Sometimes give your services for nothing, calling to mind a previous benefaction or present satisfaction. If there is an opportunity of serving a stranger in financial straits, then give full assistance. For where there is love of humanity, there is also love of the art. For some patients, though conscious that there condition is perilous; recover their health simply through their contentment with the goodness of the physician. It is important to take care of the sick to make them well, to care for the healthy to keep them well, and also to care for one's own self *(Hippocrates – Precepts 6)*.

Transformation / Personal Growth & Power

True Life Story / Bob Lumbers

"It can sometimes be so painfully obvious, but also liberating when one sees the truth and has inner courage to walk through the sorrow. For the warming energy of unconditional love and self-acceptance is waiting for you to embrace your own unique human experience. This is called life" – Bob Lumbers

The above quote is my own and brings me inspiration in life, since it is a perspective that I live by, that sheds light on situations by bringing deeper insight and clarity.
Also, I would like to say that my favourite place to be in the entire world is in the *present;* for we cannot live in the regret of the past 'nor the promise of the future. We have a chance for a new, positive direction and focus each day when we connect to the Universal energy of Love that surrounds us all.

I am anticipating that the best is yet to come. This awesome human experience I am living is an adventure to enjoy and grow with. Stumbles and set backs are the Universe's way of reminding me that I am human and can still evolve as a growing, emotionally vulnerable human being.
   - Peace, **Bob Lumbers,** Peterborough, Ontario (Canada)

Quotes: Transformation / Personal Growth & Power

- I believe that love is the main key to open the doors to the "growth" of man. Love and union with someone or something outside of oneself, union that allows one to put oneself into relationship with others, to feel one with others, without limiting the sense of integrity and independence *(Erich Fromm, Credo, 1965).*

- The meeting of two personalities is like the contact of two chemical substances: if there is any reaction, both are transformed *(Carl Jung, Modern Man in Search of a Soul, 1933, p. 49).*

- The spirit of self-help is the root of all genuine growth in the individual (*Samuel Smiles, Self Help*, 1859).

- No laws, however stringent, can make the idle industrious, the thriftless provident, or the drunken sober. Such reforms can only be affected by means of individual action, economy and self-denial; by better habits, rather than by greater rights (Samuel Smiles, *Self Help, 1859*).

- Personal power is the ability to take action *(Anthony Robbins)*.

- You will either step forward into growth, or you will step backward into safety *(Abraham Maslow)*.

- Every setback has been an education to learn from. Every success, though modest, has been a motivator to improve *(Amitabh Bachchan, Mint Lounge, "40 Years of Amitabh" by Sanjukta Sharma)*.

- You see, it's never the environment; it's never the events of our lives, but the meaning we attach to the events— how we interpret them— that shapes who we are today and who we'll become tomorrow *(Anthony Robbins)*.

- Personal power is the ability to take action *(Anthony Robbins)*.

- It is not the mountain we conquer, but ourselves *(Edmund Hillary, That's Life : Wild Wit & Wisdom, 2003 by Bonnie Louise Kuchler, p. 20)*.

- We need to be the change we wish to see in the world *(Mahatma Gandhi)*.

- You have to let it all go, Neo. Fear, doubt, and disbelief. Free your mind *(Morpheus, The Matrix)*.

- Seek not to change the world, but choose to change your mind about the world *(A Course in Miracles, 2007, p. 445)*.

- Every event has a purpose and every setback its lesson. Failure, whether of the personal, professional or even spiritual kind, is essential to personal expansion *(Robin Sharma, The Monk Sold His Ferrari, 1998)*.

- Most of us are anxious to improve our circumstances, but are unwilling to improve ourselves—and we therefore remain bound *(James Allen, As a Man Thinketh, 1902)*.

- We can lift ourselves out of ignorance, we can find ourselves as creatures of excellence and intelligence and skill *(Richard Bach, Jonathan Livingston Seagull, 1970)*.

- To truly know the world, look deeply within your own being; to truly know yourself, take real interest in the world *(Rudolph Steiner, Verses and Meditations)*.

Trust / Faith

True Life Story by Wanda Morgan

Making decisions in life can be difficult. I live by two quotes. These Biblical quotes inspire me, give me strength and make life easier for me. "Love the LORD YOUR GOD with all your soul, might and strength and love your neighbour as yourself." "I can do everything through HIM who gives me strength."

For many different reasons some people are difficult. To love difficult people is not an easy task. The love of GOD which dwells within us teaches us to be patient and loving to each other no matter our differences.

Helping each other is a way of showing love. Practising love each day by doing the little things of life will help us to be better persons. Letting someone into your lane while driving your car, picking up something for someone, a welcome smile, opening doors for a handicapped person are little things of life we should keep in mind.

There are many reasons why these things are not practical anymore.

Setting goals on a daily basis will help us to become more valuable and better persons to our society.

There are rude people out there. Being nice just to nice people doesn't give us any reward. For this reason practising love with difficult people is a virtue; a virtue that needs to be cultivated. We cannot do it on our own strengths. The quote "I can do everything through HIM who gives me strength" needs to be part of our being.

Meditation and prayers should become part of our daily life. When we ask GOD in prayers, HE will teach us patience, love and whatever we need from HIM. GOD IS LOVE. By having a close relationship with GOD on a daily basis we will cultivate these virtues and we will find it easy to say "I can do everything through him who gives me strength."
- Contributed by **Wanda Morgan**, Ontario, Canada

Quotes on Trust / Faith

- Faith is a dark night for man, but in this very way it gives him light *(St. John of the Cross, Ascent of Mt. Carmel, Bk. 2. Ch. 3. #4).*

- We are afraid of losing what we have, whether it's our life or our possessions and property. But this fear evaporates when we understand that our life stories and the history of the world were written by the same hand *(Paulo Coelho, The Alchemist, page 76).*

- There is only that moment, and the incredible certainty that everything under the sun has been written by one hand only. It is the hand that evokes love, and creates a twin soul for every person in that world. Without such love, one's dreams would have no meaning *(Paulo Coelho, The Alchemist, p. 98).*

- Preserve me, O God: for in thee do I put my trust *(Psalm 16:1).*

- The essence of faith is fewness of words and abundance of deeds *(Baha'ullah).*

WATER

"I Will"

Intuitional

- Thoughts mixed with definiteness of purpose, persistence, and burning desires are powerful things (*Napoleon Hill, The Law of Success, 1937*).

In this chapter the qualities of Water are highlighted, where you get in touch with your Willpower. With the element of Water you experience courage, flexibility, adaptability, and the subconscious. Also, you learn to enhance your creative energies, maturity and develop your character. You intone "I Will" based on focusing your energies through Willpower, and your important expressions of this element such as creativity and manifesting in physical reality. As you read the quotes related to the element Water, get in touch with creating a free flowing energy that translates spiritual concepts into actions highlighted throughout the collection of topics and true life stories in this chapter.

The Water domain asks that we become self-accepting, flowing, and yielding, along with intuitive, relaxed, patient, focused, and also to re-connect with our inner centre of power. Walt Disney captures the principle of creativity, courage, and Willpower with the following quote:

"All our dreams can come true – if we have the courage to pursue them".

Acceptance / Harmony / Balance / Centeredness / Grounding / Moderation

"Without mutual respect there is only strife and confusion. To find balance, we must find a clear perspective of the entire issue at hand, without personal prejudice." (Bret Varcado, Sacramento, California - U.S., Original Quote).

- Every experience that you have and will have upon the Earth encourages the alignment of your personality with your soul *(Gary Zukav, The Seat of the Soul, 1990)*.

- One must marry one's feelings to one's beliefs and ideas. That is probably the only way to achieve a measure of harmony in one's life *(Napoleon Hill, The Law of Success, 1937)*.

- I've learned that you can't have everything and do everything at the same time *(Oprah Winfrey, O Magazine, April 2003)*.

- Do not be too hard, lest you be broken; do not be too soft, lest you be squeezed *(Imam Ali)*.

- To everything there is a season, and a time to every purpose under heaven: A time to be born, and a time to die; a time to plant, and a time to uproot what is planted. A time to kill, and a time to heal; a time to break down, and a time to build up; A time to weep, and a time to laugh; a time to mourn, and a time to dance; A time to cast away stones, and a time to gather stones together; a time to embrace, and a time to refrain from embracing; A time to seek, and a time to lose; a time to keep, and a time to cast away; A time to rend, and a time to sew; a time to keep silence, and a time to speak; A time to love, and a time to hate; a time for war, and a time for peace *(Ecclesiastes 3:1-8)*.
-
- Wealth does not excite me, and misfortune does not disturb me *(Guru Arjan Dev, Guru Granth Sahib, 215-1)*.

- Not exalting the gifted prevents quarrelling. Not collecting treasures prevents stealing. Not seeing desirable things prevents confusion of the heart *(Lao Tzu, Tao Te Ching 3)*.

- Giving birth and nourishing. Bearing yet not possessing. Working yet not taking credit. Leading yet not dominating. This is the primal virtue *(Lao Tzu, Tao Te Ching 10)*.

- Thirty spokes share the wheel's hub. It is the centre hole that makes it useful. Shape clay into a vessel. It is the space within that makes it useful. Cut doors and windows for a room. It is the holes which make it useful. Therefore benefit comes from what is there. Usefulness from what is not there *(Lao Tzu, Tao Te Ching 11)*.

- Just as a solid rock is not shaken by the storm, even so the wise are not affected by praise or blame. *(The Buddha, Dhammapada 81)*.

- We are all strangers in a strange land, longing for home, but not quite knowing what or where home is *(Madeleine L'Engle, The Rock That is Higher: Story as Truth, 1993)*.

- It is not our part to master all the tides of the world, but to do what is in us for the succour of those years wherein we are set, uprooting the evil in the fields that we know, so that those who live after may have clean earth to till. What weather they shall have is not ours to rule – Gandalf *(J.R.R. Tolkien, The Return of the King, 913)*.

- Ne quid minis – Moderation in all things *(Terence, Andria I: 61)*.

- We must adjust to changing times and still hold to unchanging principles *(Jimmy Carter quoting his teacher Julia Coleman, Nobel Lecture, Oslo, December 10, 2002)*.

- You will never be able to love anyone else until you love yourself. Even With you Fat Thighs! *(Leo Buscaglia, Speaking of Love, 1980)*.

- Distress and worry ordinarily makes things worse and even does harm to the soul itself. The endurance of all with equanimity not only reaps many blessings but also helps the soul to employ the proper remedy *(St. John of the Cross, Ascent of Mt. Carmel, Bk. 3. Ch. 6. #3)*.

- The foundation of all mental illness is the avoidance of true suffering *(Carl Jung)*.

- One day, my mother said to me, "If you become a soldier, you will be a general; if you become a monk you'll end up as the pope." Instead, I became a painter and now I am Picasso - *Mi madre un día me dijo: "Si te haces soldado, serás General; si te haces monje, terminarás como el Papa." En cambio, me hice pintor y ahora soy Picass (Pablo Picasso)*.

- The first to be summoned to Paradise on the Day of Resurrection will be those who praise God in prosperity and adversity *(Prophet Muhammad, Al-Tirmidhi, Hadith 730)*.

- Pain is part of being alive, and we need to learn that. Pain does not last forever, nor is it necessarily unbearable, and we need to be taught that *(Harold Kushner)*.

- We cannot change anything unless we accept it. Condemnation does not liberate, it oppresses *(Carl Jung)*.

When the day is done
Down to earth then sinks the sun
Along with everything that was lost and won
When the day is done *(Nick Drake, "Day is Done")*.

When I find myself in times of trouble, mother Mary comes to me, speaking words of wisdom, let it be *(Beatles, Let It Be, 1970, "Let It Be")*.

- Life is a series of natural and spontaneous changes. Don't resist them – that only creates sorrow. Let reality be reality. Let things flow naturally forward in whatever way they like *(Lao Tzu, Wisdom for the Soul: Five Millennia of Prescriptions for the Soul, 2006, p. 22)*.

- He who submits to fate without complaint is wise *(Euripides, Wisdom for the Soul: Five Millennia of Prescriptions for the Soul, 2006, p. 22)*.

- The greatest devotion, greater than learning and praying, consists in accepting the world exactly as it happens to be *(Hasidic saying)*.

- Flow with whatever is happening and let your mind be free *(Chuang Tzu, The Law of Attraction: Making It Work For You, 2009, p. 195)*.

- Seek not that the things which happen should happen as you wish; but wish the things which happen to be as they are, and you will have a tranquil flow of life *(Epictetus, Enchiridion VIII)*.

- Make the best of what is in our power, and take the rest as it naturally happens *(Epictetus, The Discourses, I:1)*.

- For after all, the best thing one can do when it's raining is to let it rain *(Henry Wadsworth Longfellow, "The Birds of Killingworth," Tales of a Wayside Inn, 1863, p. 203)*.

- Acceptance of what has happened is the first step in overcoming the consequence of any misfortune *(William James quoted in How Jesus Heals Our Minds Today by David Seabury, p. 214)*.

- We win half the battle when we make up our minds to take the world as we find it, including the thorns (Orison Swett Marden, *Cheerfulness As a Life Power*, 1899, p. 67).

- Rowing against the tide is hard and uncertain. To go with the tide and thus take advantage of the workings of the great natural force is safe and easy *(Ralph Waldo Trine, The Life Books: Vol. 3: This Mystical Life of Ours, p. 74).*

- We cannot change anything unless we accept it. Condemnation does not liberate, it oppresses *(Carl Jung, Psychological Reflections, 1953).*

- Some things are in our control and others not. Things in our control are opinion, pursuit, desire, aversion, and, in a word, whatever are our own actions. Things not in our control are body, property, reputation, command, and, in one word, whatever are not our own actions. *(Epictetus, The Enchiridion 1).*

- Acceptance is not submission; it is acknowledgement of the facts of the situation. Then deciding what you're going to do about it *(M. Kathleen Casey).*

- Acceptance is the answer to all my problems today...I can find no serenity until I accept that person, place, thing, or situation as being exactly the way it is supposed to be *(Alcoholics Anonymous).*

- Accept – then act. Whatever the present moment contains, accept it as if you had chosen it. Always work with it, not against it *(Eckhard Tolle, The Power of Now: A Guide to Spiritual Enlightenment, 1999).*

- Accept what comes to you totally and completely so that you can appreciate it, learn from it, and then let it go *(Deepak Chopra, Journey Into Healing: Awakening the Wisdom Within You, 1994).*

- Once we truly know that life is difficult – then life is no longer difficult. Because once it is accepted, the fact that life is difficult no longer matters *(M. Scott Peck, The Road Less Travelled, 1978).*

- A serene acceptance of what is promotes health, but by keeping the mind clear it also puts a person in a better position to change things that need changing *(Bernie Siegal, Love, Medicine & Miracles, 1986)*.

- Peace of mind comes from not wanting to change others, but by simply accepting them as they are. True acceptance is always without demands and expectations *(Gerald Jampolsky, Love is Letting Go of Fear, 1979)*.

Desire / Drives / Passions / Pleasures / Will

- One of humanity's prime drives is to understand and be understood *(Buckminster Fuller, Operating Manual for Spaceship Earth (1963)*.

- If you have the ability to desire it, the Universe has the ability to deliver it. You've just got to line up with what you want, which means— be as happy as you can be *(Abraham-Hicks)*.

- The soul that is clouded by the desires is darkened in the understanding and allows neither the sun of natural reason nor that of the supernatural Wisdom of God to shine upon it and illumine it clearly.... Darkness and coarseness will always be with a soul until its appetites are extinguished. The appetites are like a cataract on the eye or specks of dust in it; until removed they obstruct vision. The affections and appetites deprive them of a treasure of divine light *(St. John of the Cross, Ascent of Mt. Carmel, Bk. 1. Ch. 8)*.

- You desire and do not have; so you kill. And you covet and cannot obtain; so you fight and wage war. You do not have, because you do not ask. You ask and do not receive, because you ask wrongly, to spend it on your passions *(James 4:1-3)*.

- The soul of the lazy desires and gets nothing; but the soul of the hard-working is satisfied *(Proverbs 13:4)*.

- The hunger of the hungry is not appeased, even by piling up loads of worldly goods *(Guru Nanak, Guru Granth Sahib, 1-5)*.

- Ever desireless, one can see the mystery. Ever desiring, one can see the manifestations *(Lao Tzu, Tao Te Ching 2)*.

- Just as rain breaks through an ill-thatched house, so passion penetrates an undeveloped mind. *(Budhha, The Dhammapada13)*.

- There is no crime greater than having too many desires. There is no disaster greater than not being content *(Lao Tzu, Tao Te Ching 46)*.

- There is a sufficiency in the world for man's need but not for man's greed *(Mahatma Gandhi)*.

- When you want something, all the universe conspires in helping you to achieve it *(Paulo Coelho, The Alchemist, page 22)*.

- Pleasure is the beginning and end of living happily *(Epicurus, From Lives of Eminent Philosophers by Diogenes Laertius)*.

- No pleasure is itself a bad thing, but the things that produce some kinds of pleasure, bring along with them dissatisfaction that is much greater than the pleasure itself *(Epicurus, Sovereign Maxims 8)*.

- You can have anything you want – if you want it badly enough. You can be anything you want to be, do anything you set out to accomplish if you hold to that desire with singleness of purpose *(Abraham Lincoln)*.

- Champions aren't made in gyms. Champions are made from something they have deep inside them – a desire, a dream, a vision. They have to have the skill, and the will. But the will must be stronger than the skill *(Muhammad Ali)*.

- Keep a tight rein on desire, but do not give up desire altogether *(Vishnu Sharma, Panchatantra, II. 58)*.

- The passions are like fire, useful in a thousand ways and dangerous only in one, through their excess *(Christian Bovee, Thoughts, Feelings and Fancies, 1857)*.

Determination / Courage / Strength / Motivation / Willpower

- The difference between a big shot and a little shot is that a big shot's just a little shot that kept on shooting *(Zig Ziglar)*.

- I think your job is just to be there 100% - you work hard and there are no shortcuts to success *(Preity Zinta)*.

- The season of failure is the best time for sowing the seeds of success *(Paramahansa Yogananda)*.

- You gain strength, courage and confidence by every experience in which you really stop to look fear in the face *(Eleanor Roosevelt, You Learn By Living, Foreword, 1960, p. 29 – 30)*.

- One must never, for whatever reason, turn his back on life *(Eleanor Roosevelt, Preface, December 1960 to The Autobiography of Eleanor Roosevelt, 1961, p. xix)*.

- Whenever a person rises from one level to the next, it necessitates that he first has a descent before the ascent. Because the purpose of any descent is always in order to ascend *(Nachman of Breslov, LM 22)*.

- Victory belongs to the most persevering *(Napoléon Bonaparte)*.

- Happy is the man who avoids dissension, but how fine is the man who is afflicted and shows endurance *(Sunah of Abu Dawood, Hadith 1996)*.

- I had an acting teacher who once told me that you could never really create from comfort. To do well as an actress, you have to push yourself to the edge *(Salma Hayek, Interview with Oprah Winfrey in O magazine, "Passion," September 2003)*.

- I know of no more encouraging fact than the unquestionable ability of man to elevate his life by a conscious endeavour *(Henry David Thoreau, Walden, 1854)*.

- It's not whether you get knocked down; it's whether you get up *(Vince Lombardi)*.

- Effort only fully releases its reward after a person refuses to quit *(Napoleon Hill, The Law of Success, 1937, p. 109)*.

- It is not eminent talent that is required to ensure success in any pursuit, so much as purpose—not merely the power to achieve, but the will to labour energetically and perseveringly. Hence energy of will may be defined to be the very central power of character in a man *(Samuel Smiles, Self Help, 1859)*.

- Warriors strive to be strong, to have an impact upon the world, and to avoid ineffectiveness and passivity *(Carol S. Pearson, The Hero Within)*.

- Determine that the thing can and shall be done, and then we shall find the way *(Abraham Lincoln, Speech in the House of Representatives, 20 June 1848)*.

- I command you: be strong and steadfast! Do not fear nor be dismayed, for the Lord, your God, is with you wherever you go *(Joshua 1:9)*.

- God is our refuge and strength, a very present help in trouble. Therefore will not we fear, though the earth be removed, and though the mountains be carried into the midst of the sea *(Psalm 46:1-2)*.

- When one has nothing to lose, one becomes courageous. We are timid only when there is something we can cling to *(Carlos Castaneda, The Wheel of Time, 2001, p. 161).*

Discipline / Self-Control / Mastery

- Silence and Self-control is non-violence *(Mahavira).*

- I never could have done what I have done, without the habits of punctuality, order, and diligence, without the determination to concentrate myself on one object at a time *(Charles Dickens, David Copperfield, 1850, Chapter 42).*

- What are these tools, these techniques of suffering, these means of experiencing the pain of problems constructively that I call discipline? There are four: delaying of gratification, acceptance of responsibility, dedication to truth, and balancing ... they are simple tools, and almost all children are adept in their use by the age of ten. Yet presidents and kings will often forget to use them, to their downfall *(M. Scott Peck, The Road Less Travelled, 1978).*

- Without discipline we can solve nothing. With only some discipline we can solve only some problems. With total discipline we can solve all problems *(M. Scott Peck, The Road Less Travelled, 1978).*

Challenges / Adversity / Overcoming / Suffering / Pain

True Life Story by **Raj Kamal**

Nanak Dukhiya Sab Sansaar – Nanak says: The whole world is suffering **– Guru Nanak**, Ramkali, M1, 945-5)

This quote is from "Guru Granth Sahib Ji" (Sikh holy book), which means everyone has his/her own problems, it's just that you feel your problems are bigger than others. But when you get to know other's problems you realize that your problems are smaller or simpler to solve.

I apply this in my own life by devotional service to other people. When you give to others in whatever capacity, you realize that you have something unique to give. In helping others, whether serving a meal to someone, giving time or money to charity or helping out at your place of worship allows you to get beyond your own suffering.

You learn that all of us suffer in different ways and that through compassion we can help each other. Whenever you connect to something bigger than you, then you can arise above the sense of suffering, pain, sorrow or dissatisfaction. So devote yourself to sincere devotion, compassion and service and you will find that as you help another, you are also changed.
- Contributed by
  Raj Kamal, Ontario, Canada

True Life Story by Michael Richards

"Sometimes the worst of times brings out the best in people"
- **Michael Richards**, June 2008

On Friday the 13th, 2008, one of the largest disasters in U.S. history placed 10 square miles of the downtown and core residential neighbourhoods of Cedar Rapids, Iowa under water. 25,000 people were evacuated. 5,000 National Guard Troops cordoned off the entire centre of the city to keep people out of harm's way as a massive 32 foot wall of water surged through the City. Amazingly, not a single person died, and only minor injuries were reported during these days of unprecedented disaster. There was no loss of life, but the loss of property was immense; thousands of homes, a thousand businesses and scores of churches and schools were utterly destroyed. Even during the deep economic recession that gripped the nation in 2008, the people of Cedar Rapids now had a 5 billion dollar additional financial burden to bear.

For three days before this immense flood, thousands of citizen volunteers worked around the clock building sandbag and earthen levees in their last ditch common effort to shield homes and business buildings from the cresting waters. Sand bag walls were built several feet higher than the water levels of the largest previous floods in history. The massive surge overcame this heroic human effort, as a 32 foot wall of water pushed the sandbags aside and destroyed everything in its wake. Even after families saw their own homes and possessions flushed away, thousands still banded together to protect key common assets of the City. Three of the four City water pump stations had already been submerged in the flood. A thousand people gathered in torrential rain and waded in waist deep at rivers' edge to build an immense sand bag structure to save the *4th and final city water well*. As that impossible task was made possible with the unified action of thousands of hands, the call rang through the crowd that flood waters were now pouring into the main floor entrance of a regional hospital a few miles away on the other side of the river. Without stopping to rest, this army of volunteers jumped into cars and pick-up trucks to build a human chain to pass sand bags around the entire perimeter of the hospital. The flood waters rose quicker than the sand bags. An emergency call went out for ambulances to come in from nearby towns, and even the adjacent states of Wisconsin and Illinois, to carry out one of the largest hospital evacuations in history. The volunteer's sandbagging kept a path open until the last patient was loaded into the last ambulance. The army of volunteers quickly retreated to higher ground as the flood waters pushed on in.

Five blocks away from the hospital, the homes of Michael and Lynette Richards and the homes of four of their adult sons were taking the full brunt of the deepest flood waters. Their family business building was also fully submerged, destroying twenty years of family business effort. This was especially ironic, as for several years previous to this disaster, the Richards family had been driving vans of volunteers to help rebuild along the Gulf Coast after Katrina. Now the Richards were on the other end of disaster, as victims rather than volunteers. From day one, the Richards *never defined themselves as victims; they are a family of very resilient survivors.*

They stood in line with thousands of other families made homeless by the flood to receive food, water, clothing and basic necessities to start building their lives back up from scratch, one step at a time. This huge flood hit so fast and furious that most of the 25,000 people evacuated only took what they had on their back, and what they could each carry in one suitcase, bag or box.

The Richards had the experience of their time helping people rebuild after Katrina. They were now called into action to help people on their own block in their own neighbourhood. The Governor selected Michael Richards to serve on the State-wide Economic Recovery Task Force; Rebuild Iowa. Lynette was appointed by the Cedar Rapids school system to help hundreds of students and their families find housing and to rebuild the fabric of their daily lives. Michael Richards was appointed as a citizen/neighbourhood liaison to the City/County Recovery and Re-Investment Co-ordinating Team. For months after the flood, the Richards led the "Block Brigades" where a hundred or so neighbours worked together a block at a time to clear out flood debris with manual labour. Lynette is an excellent cook and Michael is a citizen activist, neighbourhood organizer, so they worked as a team to get a truckload of food donated each week to prepare a community feast and celebration to feed a hot home cooked meal to hundreds of disaster recovery volunteers. These community meals built a strong sense of connection and purpose.

As their neighbourhood and community service has been rendered non-stop for three years since the flood, the Richards family have also rebuilt their own four homes and business building after the disaster. The best word to describe the Richards' family is "resilience". *Resilience* is defined as a "capacity for systems to absorb disturbance and re-organize while undergoing change, retaining essentially their same function, structure, identity and key information exchange".

The Richards have not just re-built. They are re-building with an understanding of their place in the community and the local ecology. They now have raised homes on higher foundations above the flood plain. They have recovered and recycled tons of building materials from homes that were bulldozed after the flood ... this has yielded historic wood flooring, woodwork and bevelled glass windows for five comfortable and attractive family homes. They have a cluster of intergenerational homes in a village setting with shared gardens, root cellars, rain water collection and a starter greenhouse; this functions as a small intentional community; *Oakleaf Village.*

Michael Richards is the author of *Sustainable Operating Systems/The Post Petrol Paradigm.* *The Richards family are modeling a sustainable lifestyle as they re-build from an ecological disaster.* Climate change, the way we utilize non-renewable resources, the way farmland is managed and the way cities are built with miles and miles of pavement all combine to create situations where rainwater that used to be absorbed by the natural environment now rush to rivers and streams unabated.

"Natural Disasters" such as Katrina and the Iowa Flood of 2008 are caused or at the least made much worse by human action. The State

Archaeologist of Iowa stated that there was no previous evidence in 7,500 years of Native American settlement in this river valley that water had ever raised this high. We need to discover better ways to live within our natural environment. The Richards are engaged in an effort to find such better ways.

Three years after the Flood of 2008, The Governor of Iowa cited Michael and Lynette Richards for exceptional community service in disaster recovery.

"Sometimes the worst of times brings out the very best in people."

-Michael Richards, June 2008

Winner of Award from Governor General of Iowa
319-213-2051
soyawax@aol.com

The Post Disaster Context
Oakhill-Jackson/New Bohemia Neighbourhood Garden:

For 10 years a growing green space in the heart of the new Bohemia Art and Cultural District has served as a lively vortex of neighbourhood communication and shared community action. *The Oakhill-Jackson/New Bohemia Neighbourhood Garden* started in 2000 in the backyard behind the *Historic Matyk Building* at 1029 Third St. S. E. In that first Spring of 2001, a dozen or so immigrant youth that lived with their families at Osada one block to the North gathered at the empty lot to work with Matyk Building owners, Michael and Lynette Richards. They hauled in loads of fertile soil, tilled the ground and planted a variety of garden produce seeds. Everyone helped to cultivate and nurture the garden. Neighbourhood kids and families gathered throughout that first summer to cook and grill next to the growing garden. Produce was shared with Osada families and other Oakhill neighbours all summer long. We celebrated Fall with a block party and cookout.

During the following years, every Spring Osada kids would knock on the Richards' family apartment door at the side of The Matyk

Building. This Spring planting tradition went on for several years. Other neighbours up and down Third Street and Second Street joined in each year. On many summer nights friends and neighbours set up a projector and presented neighbourhood movies on the side wall of the Matyk Building. The garden effort grew into adjacent backyards. At our neighbourhood block party every Spring various households up and down our shared back alley decided who would plant which varieties of produce. Everyone grew different things, and we all shared produce each summer... -*until the Flood of 2008 washed the community garden and all of our homes away. The entire block of 10 homes were totally destroyed.* The only surviving structure still in use on our block now is the Historic Matyk Building. The lot just to the North, where the home of Michael Richards Jr. and his wife Liza had once stood now provides additional space for a larger expanded garden. In the Summer of 2009, our community garden was again planted as an expression of family and neighbourhood *resilience*. A garden is a great way to re-build and re-group after a major disaster.

After the flood, the Richards family has continued to donate the use of garden land. They've worked with *Americorps-Greencorps* to plant and provide healthy food to low income families and flood survivors. In 2011, students in the *Kirkwood Community College Horticulture program* are lending their skilled hands and open hearts to the effort. The garden has no fence and is open to all to come and share. Homeless men and women wander through the community garden and pick fresh food on many days.

To expand the garden effort, for several years, the Richards family have co-ordinated *a local food initiative* where at-risk inner city youth partner with Iowa Amish Farm families to bring healthy food to low income single moms, at risk youth, the elderly and others in nee. This neighbourhood food initiative has expanded to include surplus food gleaned from C.S.A. farms in Linn and Johnson County, as well as surplus eggs, cheese, milk, and butter from Kalona organics. A local bakery provides a hundred or more loaves of bread each week. We intend to keep this community garden effort growing as a long term project; we have additional garden lots available nearby for the coming season in 2012.

For 2011, we concentrated our effort at 1029 Third St. S. E.

It is important for all of us to participate in open circles of both giving and receiving. Many of the folks in the neighbourhood that receive food also volunteer to give back as they plant, weed and harvest in our neighbourhood garden. Many of these same families also go along with Lynette to offer volunteer labour at the farms that generously donate food. Literally tons of food is shared each month. All of this operates with *no formal funding source, just the shared time and effort of a vital neighbourhood.* If you have a church group, a youth group or community service group that would like to assist with this growing effort, we have an *open volunteer day at 10 a.m. each and every Saturday.* The first open volunteer day will take place this year on Saturday April 2, 2011. On that first open volunteer day we will have a few dozen shovels and rakes to clear out old growth, till the ground and put down new wood chips on the garden paths. We will then meet at 10 a.m. every Saturday until the garden is thriving and to keep it weeded and kept up. We hope to see you on Saturday, April 2nd, or any following Saturday during this season that works for you.

For further information, you can call us,
Michael & Lynette Richards
<u>319-213-2051.</u>

- Contributed by **Michael Richards**
  soyawax@aol.com

Michael Richards is a lifelong *Innovator, Entrepreneur, and Author.* His company *Soyawax International* is the recognized originator of the growing market shift from Petroleum Wax to Soy wax in several industries.

Michael Richards is Author of two books:
"Light One Candle" and *"Sustainable Operating Systems"* are presently available at www.amazon.com

Michael Richards is releasing four new books in 2012.

Quotes on Challenges / Adversity / Overcoming / Suffering / Pain

- In a real dark night of the soul it is always three o'clock in the morning, day after day *(F. Scott Fitzgerald, The Crack-Up, 1936).*

- This dark night is an inflowing of God into the soul *(St. John of the Cross, The Dark Night of the Soul, Bk 2, Ch.5, #1).*

- However vast the darkness, we must supply our own light *(Stanley Kubrick, Interviewed by Eric Nordern, Playboy, September 1968).*

- Into each life some rain must fall, Some days must be dark and dreary *(Henry Wadsworth Longfellow, The Rainy Day, 1842).*

- Difficult times always create opportunities for you to experience more love in your life *(Barbara De Angelis).*

- Ignorance, egoism, attachment, aversion and fear of death are the five afflictions *(Patanjali, Aphorisms, 2: 3).*

- Challenges are gifts that force us to search for a new center of gravity. Don't fight them. Just find a different way to stand *(Oprah Winfrey, O Magazine, October 2002).*

- I have learned that success is to be measured not so much by the position that one has reached in life as by the obstacles which he has overcome while trying to succeed *(Booker T. Washington, Up From Slavery, 1901, Chapter II: Boyhood Days).*

- The tests of life are not meant to break you, but to make you *(Norman Vincent Peale).*

- The greatest glory in living lies not in never falling, but in rising every time we fall *(Nelson Mandela, Long Walk to Freedom, 1995)*.

- No one can go through life without their share of knocks. I am no different from any other *(Amitabh Bachchan)*.

- We may encounter many defeats but we must not be defeated *(Maya Angelou)*.

- A happy life consists not in the absence, but in the mastery of hardships *(Helen Keller, The Simplest Way to be Happy, 1933)*.

- Every adversity carries with it the seed of an equivalent or greater benefit *(Napoleon Hill, The Law of Success, 1937)*.

- The greatest and most important problems of life are all fundamentally insoluble. They can never be solved but only outgrown *(Carl Jung)*.

- The way in which a man accepts his fate and all the suffering it entails, the way in which he takes up his cross, gives him ample opportunity — even under the most difficult circumstances — to add a deeper meaning to his life *(Viktor Frankl, Man's Search For Meaning, 1946)*.

- In a position of utter desolation, when man cannot express himself in positive action, when his only achievement may consist in enduring his sufferings in the right way — an honourable way — in such a position man can, through loving contemplation of the image he carries of his beloved, achieve fulfillment *(Viktor Frankl, Man's Search For Meaning, 1946)*.

- Suffering — how divine it is, how misunderstood! We owe to it all that is good in us, all that gives value to life; we owe to it pity, we owe to it courage, we owe to it all the virtues *(Anatole France, Le Jardin d'Épicure [Epicure's Garden], 1894)*.

- Accept suffering and achieve atonement through it — that is what you must do *(Fyodor Dostoevsky, Crime and Punishment, 1866)*.

- You are called to exercise the Spirit's gifts amidst the ups and downs of your daily life *(Pope Benedict XVI, World Youth Day 2008, held in Australia, Youth Day Vigil, 19/07/08)*.

- As Benjamin Franklin said, 'Those things that hurt, instruct.' It is for this reason that wise people learn not to dread but actually to welcome problems and actually to welcome the pain of problems. *(M. Scott Peck, The Road Less Travelled, 1978)*.

- Pain is the medicine while comfort is the disease *(Guru Nanak)*.

- From struggle comes strength. Even pain can be a wonderful teacher *(Robin Sharma, The Monk Who Sold His Ferrari, 1999)*.

- I have learned that success is to be measured not so much by the position that one has reached in life as by the obstacles which he has overcome while trying to succeed *(Booker T. Washington, Up From Slavery: An Autobiography, 2007, p. 31)*.

- Though I walk through the valley of the shadow of death, I will fear no evil: for thou art with me *(Psalm 23:4)*.

- If gold must be gold, it must pass through the furnace *(T.B. Joshua, "Bewitching Favour," Africa News, September 22, 2009)*.

- Difficulties strengthen the mind, as labour does the body *(Seneca)*.

- Face adversity promptly and without flinching, and you will reduce its impact *(Winston Churchill quoted in Wisdom for the Soul by Larry Chang, 2006, p. 38)*.

- We could never learn to be brave and patient if there were only joy in the world *(Helen Keller, The Story of My Life, 2007, p. 88)*.

- Be grateful even for hardship, setbacks, and bad people. Dealing with such obstacles is an essential part of training in the Art of Peace *(Morihei Ueshiba & John Stevens, The Art of Peace, 2002, p. 76)*.

- We learn as much from sorrow as from joy, as much from illness as from health, from handicap as from advantage – and indeed perhaps more *(Pearl S. Buck as quoted in Seed Sown by Jay Cormier, 1996, p. 97)*.

- We are built to conquer environment, solve problems, achieve goals, and we find no real satisfaction or happiness in life without obstacles to conquer and goals to achieve *(Maxwell Maltz, Psycho-Cybernetics, 1960)*.

- Much of the pain caused by our problems stems in part from our own unchanging biases in terms of how we interpret our personal difficulties to ourselves *(Pir Vilayat Inayat Khan, Awakening: A Sufi Experience, 1999)*.

- The ultimate measure of a man is not where he stands in moments of comfort and convenience, but where he stands at times of challenge and controversy *(Martin Luther King, Jr., Strength to Love, 1977, p. 35)*.

- Wise people learn not to dread but actually to welcome problems because it is in this whole process of meeting and solving problems that life has its meaning *(M. Scott Peck, The Road Less Travelled, 2012, p. 16)*.

- The way I see it, if you want the rainbow, you gotta put up with the rain *(Dolly Parton quoted in Confident Children by Gael Lindenfield, 2012, p. 174)*.

Encouragement / Hope

True Life Story by Hope S. Leon

I've used this theory many times in the past as an Elementary School Teacher, particularly when dealing with behavioural students, or students with various learning difficulties. In either of these cases, you're providing a 'positive' encouraging learning model. By using this confidence-building approach, it causes a complete turnaround, an obvious change in personality, behaviour, and attitude, along with a great improvement in learning skills.

One of my initial and most successful 'methods' in my bag of teaching tricks, was to **tap into** something the child *liked,* or *was good at. One of my behavioural students, for example,* **liked to be the 'BOSS',** if you know what I mean… so I made him the BOSS. I gave him a *second* desk, which he made into his own personal "office". I put him in charge of specific tasks, as "my assistant", … with responsibilities and jobs to do. Suddenly, … , gradually, the person was doing 'positive' things, and was no longer displaying negative behaviour, and getting into trouble. Instead, he was "helping others", and helping me, … with a new sense of pride, and accomplishment.

A very shy, quiet student in on of my grade three classes, had always had panic attacks, and all sorts of fears related to school throughout the years. I noticed instantly the first day when she arrived in class, that she was **very creative,** so I tapped into her "artsiness" (like me), … her creativity, love of colour, and design etc. I had her show me *her* creations, and Vice Versa. We bonded instantly. I didn't force her, but gave her the *confidence* to try new things, and gradually she did. By Christmas, she actually performed in our Christmas assembly, in front of the entire school, which was a first! I was very proud of her, as was her Mom, and she was terrific. At the end of the school year, she gave me a gift which I treasure to this day. She gave me three tiny garden rocks … you know … the ones with "inspirational" words on them. The words she chose were three words she told me, … that "I had given her": 1) Confidence 2)

Love 3) Imagination. The rocks are outside on my front garden bed, ... and I treasure them, knowing they came from her.

So that's what I mean by what that quote can accomplish. If people are lead to believe they are failures, ... they will fail. If they are lead to believe they are lead to believe they can accomplish great things ... they will!

- Contributed by
 Hope S. Leon, *Retired Elementary School Teacher,* Hamilton, Ontario (Canada)

Quotes on Encouragement / Hope

- When a person falls from his level he should know that it's heaven-sent, because going down is needed in order to go up *(Nachman of Breslov, LM 261).*

- Life is one big road with lots of signs. So when you riding through the ruts, don't complicate your mind *(Bob Marley).*

- We may encounter many defeats but we must not be defeated *(Maya Angelou).*

- Remember, Hope is a good thing, maybe the best of things, and no good thing ever dies *(Rita Hayworth and Shawshank Redemption).*

- Failure is the opportunity to begin again more intelligently *(Henry Ford).*

- I'd like to think, eight years ago, I was pretty humble and modest. But I think, with each year, you get more modest, more humble, more appreciative. The off the field tragedies put things in better perspective, but life happens to everybody, and I think we all just try to do the best we can *(Brett Favre).*

- All of us failed to match our dreams of perfection. So I rate us on the basis of our splendid failure to do the impossible *(William Faulkner, Interview in Writers at Work, 1958)*. The glory of life is not ever falling. The true glory consists in rising each time we fall *(Chinmayananda)*.

- No tribal rite has yet been recorded which attempts to keep winter from descending; on the contrary: the rites all prepare the community to endure, together with the rest of nature, the season of the terrible cold *(Joseph Campbell, The Hero with a Thousand Faces, 1949, Chapter 2)*.

- Truth is the light. So you never give up the fight *(Bob Marley, Final jamming of Live at the Roxy, recorded 1976)*.

- Get up, stand up, Stand up for your rights. Get up, stand up, Don't give up the fight *(Bob Marley, "Get Up, Stand Up," Burnin' 1973)*.

- When you are in dire straits and none come to help you. When you are besieged by enemies and your relatives desert you. When you have lost all hope and help from anyone. Then set your mind on the True Lord and then no harm shall touch you. *(Guru Arjun, Guru Granth Sahib, 70-6 & 7)*.

- If you are weakened by the pains of hunger and poverty, with no money in your pockets, and no one will give you any comfort, and no one will satisfy your hopes and desires, and none of your works is accomplished. If you then come to remember the Supreme Lord, you shall obtain the eternal kingdom *(Guru Arjan Dev, Guru Granth Sahib, 70:9-10)*.

- The birds have no money in their pockets. They place their hopes on trees and water. Their provider is only one *(Guru Nanak Dev, Guru Granth Sahib, 144:4)*.

- The world is indeed full of peril, and in it there are many dark places; but still there is much that is fair, and though in all lands love is now mingled with grief, it grows perhaps the greater – Haldir *(J.R.R. Tolkien, The Fellowship of the Ring, 367).*

- Hope, like faith, is nothing if it is not courageous; it is nothing if it is not ridiculous *(Thornton Wilder, The Eight Day, 1967).*

- While there's life, there's hope *(Terence, Heauton Timoroumenos I: 981).*

- And Jesus opened his mouth, and taught them, saying: "Blessed are the poor in spirit: for theirs is the kingdom of heaven. Blessed are they that mourn: for they shall be comforted. Blessed are the meek: for they shall inherit the earth. Blessed are they which do hunger and thirst after righteousness: for they shall be filled" *(Matthew 5:2-6).*

Flowing / Change / Impermanence / Emptiness / Temporality

True Life Story by Edane Padme

"In having complete trust in the Universe, I will simply go where my heart takes me and simply let go of what isn't mine." – Edane Padme (Original Quote).

This is a quote I had written after meeting a special friend, the way we met was the way of Fate. Stars perfectly aligned and my solar plexus chakra fully activated. I felt God's inhalation and the Goddess' exhalation, when my inner voice told me to "pay attention, you're life's about to change right now." My life did change. I can no longer deny the voice of my spirit guide, my intuition. I am learning to surrender to the Universe, trust that everything that happens to me is to serve a higher purpose, growth and evolution. The Universe has already planned out a journey for me and the map is written in my heart. The way to navigate is through the practice of meditation.

When I simply go where my heart takes me, my blood flows like a river, my mind is as calm as the sea, every breath is profound, my spirit flies freely and every single cell in my body is happy.

When I am living in fear and I fight against the wind, I end up damaging my soul and I am reminded of the Karmic relationships and events I need to face. I meet challenges in every direction of my life. I become sick, miserable and angry. And I won't have anyone to blame, but myself.

The root of suffering is desire, when we desire something or someone, we become attached. The end of suffering is detachment to form and the five senses (touch, smell, see, hear, taste) and instead use our sixth sense, the spirit to guide us to love.

The practice of letting go allows us and others to be free. Nothing in this world belongs to us, not your thoughts, ideas, not your children, not your husband or wife, not your clothes, not even your SOUL. The soul belongs to the Universe and yet Universe doesn't claim ownership. The Universe wants every being to be FREE.

- **Edane Padme**
  Spiritual Intuitive and Yoga Instructor
  Toronto, Canada
  www.sacredfemmes.com
  sacredfemmes@live.ca

Quotes on Flowing / Change / Impermanence / Emptiness / Temporality

• Nothing endures but change *(Heraclitus, Lives of the Philosophers by Diogenes Laertius).*

• All changes, even the most longed for, have their melancholy, for what we leave behind us is a part of ourselves; we must die to one life before we can enter into another *(Anatole France as quoted in Happy 4 Life by Bob Nozik, 2003, p. 184).*

- Things do not change; we change *(Henry David Thoreau, Walden, 1926, p. 230)*.

- However confused the scene of our life appears, however torn we may be who now do face that scene, it can be faced, and we can go on to be whole *(Muriel Rukeyeser in Transitions by Julia Cameron, 1999, p. 1)*.

- When I dance I dance; when I sleep I sleep *(Montaigne, "Experience," Essays of Montaigne, Charles Cotton, tr., 1877)*.

- Without going out of my door I can know all things on earth. Without looking out of my window I can know the ways of Heaven. The farther one travels the less one knows.... Arrive without travelling see all without looking do all without doing *(The Beatles, "The Inner Light")*.

- Like everyone else you want to learn the way to win. But never to accept the way to lose. To accept defeat — to learn to die — is to be liberated from it. Once you accept, you are free to flow and to harmonize. Fluidity is the way to an empty mind. You must free your ambitious mind and learn the art of dying *(Bruce Lee, Striking Thoughts, 2000, p. 25)*.

- *Emptiness the starting point.* — In order to taste my cup of water you must first empty your cup. My friend, drop all you preconceived and fixed ideas and be neutral. Do you know why this cup is useful? Because it is *empty (Bruce Lee, Striking Thoughts, 2000, p. 2)*.

- Wealth, the beauty of youth, and flowers are guests for only a few days *(Guru Nanak Dev, Guru Granth Sahib, 23-5)*.

- Households, mansions and wealth - whatever is seen, is like the shade of a tree *(Guru Arjan Dev, Guru Granth Sahib, 212-18)*.

- Body, wealth and youth pass away *(Guru Arjan Dev, Guru Granth Sahib, 826:6)*.

- If I were to become an emperor and raise a huge army, and sit on a throne, issuing commands and collecting taxes. O Nanak, all of this could pass away like a gust of wind *(Guru Nanak Dev, Guru Granth Sahib, 14:6)*.

As the spider sends forth and draws in its thread, as plants grow on the earth, as hair grows on the head and the body of a living person—so does everything in the universe arise from the Infinite *(Mundaka Upanishad 1.1.7)*.

- We must become the change we want to see in the world *(Mahatma Gandhi)*.|

Stop trying to control everything and just let go *(Tyler Durden, Fight Club, 1999)*.

- All major changes are like death. You can't see what is on the other side until you get there *(Dr. Ian Malcolm, Jurrasic Park)*.

- The true purpose of Zen is to see things as they are, to observe things as they are, and to let everything go as it goes. Zen practice is to open up our small mind *(Shunryu Suzuki, Zen Mind, Beginner's Mind, 1973, Prologue)*.

- When you sit, you will sit. When you eat, you will eat *(Shunryu Suzuki, Zen Mind, Beginner's Mind, 1973, p. 41)*.

- Open yourself to the Tao, then trust your natural responses, and everything will fall into place (Lao Tzu).

- Everything flows and nothing stays fixed *(Heraclitus, quoted by Plato in Cratylus)*

- You cannot step twice into the same river *(Heraclitus, quoted by Plato in Cratylus)*.

- One generation goes, and another generation comes; but the earth remains forever *(Ecclesiastes 1:4)*.

- The present life is a brief diversion and sport but the hereafter offers eternal life, if they only knew *(Quran 29:64)*.

- The life of this world is made up of three days: yesterday has gone with all that was done; tomorrow, you may never reach; but today is for you so do what you should do *today (Saint Hasan of Basra, Quoted in Al-Bayhaqi, Al-Zuhd Al-Kabîr, p.197)*.

- One who resists the wave is swept away, but one who bends before it abides *(Midrash, Genesis Rabbah 44:1)*.

- Peace originates with the flow of things – its heart is like the movement of the wind and the waves. The Way is like the veins that circulate blood through our bodies, following the natural flow of the life force *(Morihei Ueshiba, The Art of Peace, 2010, p. 38)*.

- Surrender is the simple yet profound wisdom of *yielding* to rather than *opposing* the flow of life *(Eckhard Tolle, The Power of Now: A Guide to Spiritual Enlightenment, 2010, p. 237)*.

Leadership

- Leadership means that a group, large or small, is willing to entrust authority to a person who has shown judgement, wisdom, personal appeal, and proven competence *(Walt Disney, How to Be Like Walt : Capturing the Magic Every Day of Your Life, 2004, Ch. 4 : Animated Leadership, p. 102)*.

- Real leaders ask hard questions and knock people out of their comfort zones and then manage the resulting distress *(Alan Hirsch, The Faith of Leap, 2011, p. 131)*.

Earth

"I Bless"

Self-awareness

The qualities of this chapter are focused on Earth, and you get in touch with where all the energies from Spirit, Air, Fire, and Water previously activated are now released, and bear fruit. With the element of Earth you experience nurturing, fertility, grounding and fruition. Also, you learn about the power of receptivity. You intone "I Bless" based on your re-connection to wealth, health, environment, prosperity and happiness. As you read the quotes related to the element of Earth, get in touch with your responsibility to develop character qualities that enhance the process of manifesting abundance in your life, highlighted throughout the various topics and true life stories found in this chapter.

The Earth domain asks that we become Self-aware through integrating all of the activated elements of Spirit, Air, Fire, Water, and Earth. As you balance development of Self with practical, grounded awareness, you will manifest abundance to meet all of your needs on Planet Earth.

- If you have built castles in the air, your work need not be lost; that is where they should be. Now put the foundations under them *(Henry David Thoreau, Walden, 1854)*.

- To truly know the world, look deeply within your own being; to truly know yourself, take real interest in the world *(Rudolph Steiner, Verses and Meditations)*.

Nature / Environment / Animals

- I don't think of all the misery, but of the beauty that still remains... My advice is: "Go outside, to the fields, enjoy nature and the sunshine, go out and try to recapture happiness in yourself and in God. Think of all the beauty that's still left in and around you and be happy!" *(Anne Frank, The Diary, 12 June 1942 - 1 August 1944).*

- Nature's peace will flow into you as sunshine flows into trees. The winds will blow their own freshness into you and the storms their energy, while cares will drop off like autumn leaves *(John Muir, Our National Parks, 1901).*

- Everybody needs beauty as well as bread, places to play in and pray in, where nature may heal and give strength to body and soul alike *(John Muir, The Yosemite, 1912).*

- How long can men thrive between walls of brick, walking on asphalt pavements, breathing the fumes of coal and of oil, growing, working, dying, with hardly a thought of wind, and sky, and fields of grain, seeing only machine-made beauty *(Charles Lindbergh, "Aviation, Geography, and Race," 1939, Reader's Digest, November 1939, pp. 64-67).*

- We must protect the forests for our children, grandchildren and children yet to be born. We must protect the forests for those who can't speak for themselves such as the birds, animals, fish and trees *(Qwatsinas).*

- I went to the woods because I wished to live deliberately, to front only the essential facts of life, and see if I could not learn what it had to teach, and not, when I came to die, discover that I had not lived *(Henry David Thoreau, Walden, 1854).*

- Our personal consumer choices have ecological, social, and spiritual consequences. It is time to re-examine some of our deeply held notions that underlie our lifestyles *(David Suzuki)*.

- The deepest sources of the global crisis lie inside the human personality and reflect the level of consciousness evolution of our species *(Stanislav Grof, The Cosmic Game - Explorations of the Frontiers of Human Consciousness, 1997p. 219)*.

- My mission is to create a world where we can live in harmony with nature *(Jane Goodall)*.

- For nature gives to every time and season some beauties of its own; and from morning to night, as from the cradle to the grave, is but a succession of changes so gentle and easy, that we can scarcely mark their progress *(Charles Dickens, Nicholas Nickleby, 1838-1839, Chapter 22)*.

- Because we all share this small planet earth, we have to learn to live in harmony and peace with each other and with nature. That is not just a dream, but a necessity *(Dalai Lama, Nobel Lecture, 1989)*.

- As far as we know, the Earth is the only place in the universe where there is life. Its continued survival now rests in our hands *(David Attenborough, The Living Planet, 1984, Closing lines)*.

- The greatness of a nation can be judged by the way its animals are treated *(Mahatma Gandhi)*.

- The planting of trees is the least self-centred of all that we do. It is a purer act of faith than the procreation of children *(Thornton Wilder, The Eight Day, 1967)*.

- In all things of nature there is something of the marvellous *(Aristotle, On the Parts of Animals I: 5)*.

- A tiger does not proclaim his tigritude, he pounces *(Wole Soyinka quoted in Imagining Insiders: Africa and the Question of Belonging by Mineke Schipper, 1999, p. 229)*.

- The feeling of respect for all species will help us recognize the noblest nature in ourselves *(Thich Nhat Hanh quoted in Engaged Buddhist Reader by Arnold Kotler, 1996, p. 164)*.

- The talent for being happy is appreciating and liking what you have, instead of what you don't have *(Woody Allen quoted in Telling It Like It Is by Paul Bowden, 2011, p. 14)*.

Life / Experience / Living

- You're not an owner in this life; you're just a steward *(Stephen King, Commencement Address, University of Maine, May 7, 2005)*.

- Life can only be understood backwards; but it must be lived forwards *(Søren Kierkegaard, Journals of Søren Kierkegaard, 1843)*.

- Life is a mystery to be lived, not a problem to be solved *(Søren Kierkegaard)*.

- One must never, for whatever reason, turn his back on life *(Eleanor Roosevelt, Preface, December 1960 to The Autobiography of Eleanor Roosevelt, 1961, p. xix)*.

- In the heart of the sphere of everything that keeps changing, there one thing that never changes — life *(Prem Rawat, Hong Kong, China May 6, 1990)*.

- Life is one big road with lots of signs. So when you riding through the ruts, don't complicate your mind *(Bob Marley)*.

- There is a very fine line between loving life and being greedy for it *(Maya Angelou)*.

- Life is real! Life is earnest!
  And the grave is not its goal;
  Dust thou art, to dust returnest,
  Was not spoken of the soul *(Henry Wadsworth Longfellow, A Psalm of Life, 1839, st. 2)*.

- Life is like a landscape. You live in the midst of it but can describe it only from the vantage point of distance *(Charles Lindbergh, Quoted in Lindbergh: Flight's Enigmatic Hero, 2002 by Von Hardesty)*.

- Nothing ever becomes real till it is experienced—Even a proverb is no proverb to you till your Life has illustrated it *(John Keats, Letter to George and Georgiana Keats, February 14-May 3, 1819)*.

- The web of our life is of a mingled yarn, good and ill together *(William Shakespeare, All's Well That Ends Well, Act IV)*.

- To die is poignantly bitter, but the idea of having to die without having lived is unbearable *(Erich Fromm, Man for Himself, 1947, Ch. 4)*.

- I don't feel that it is necessary to know exactly what I am. The main interest in life and work is to become someone else that you were not in the beginning. If you knew when you began a book what you would say at the end, do you think that you would have the courage to write it? What is true for writing and for a love relationship is true also for life. The game is worthwhile insofar as we don't know what will be the end *(Michel Foucault, Truth, Power, Self: An Interview with Michel Foucault, 25 October 1982)*.

- Experience is what you get while looking for something else *(Federico Fellini, I'm a Born Liar (2003) edited by Damian Pettigew "Experience")*.

- For what is life but a play in which everyone acts a part until the curtain comes down? *(Desiderius Erasmus, The Praise of Folly, 1511).*

- The great moral teachers of humanity were, in a way, artistic geniuses in the art of living *(Albert Einstein, Religion and Science: Irreconcilable?, 1948).*

- Life is like riding a bicycle. To keep your balance you must keep moving *(Albert Einstein, Letter to his son Eduard, 5 February 1930).*

- From nowhere we came, into nowhere we go. What is life? It is the flash of a firefly in the night. It is the breath of a buffalo in the wintertime. It is the little shadow which runs across the grass and loses itself in the sunset *(Crowfoot).*

- People say that what we're all seeking is a meaning for life. I don't think that's what we're really seeking. I think what we're seeking is an experience of being alive, so that our life experiences on the purely physical plane will have resonance within our own innermost being and reality, so that we actually feel the rapture of being alive. That's what it's all finally about *(Joseph Campbell and The Power of Myth with Bill Moyers PBS television series, Mystic Fire Video, 2001, Episode 2, Chapter 4).*

- We must be willing to get rid of the life we planned, so as to have the life that is waiting for us *(Joseph Campbell).*

- Reality continues to ruin my life *(Calvin, Homicidal Psycho Jungle Cat, p. 67).*

- Life overall should be more glamorous, thrill-packed, and filled with applause, don't you think?... Then again, if real life was like that, what would we watch on television? *(Calvin, The Indispensable Calvin and Hobbes, p. 94).*

One of the most tragic things I know about human nature is that all of us tend to put off living. We are all dreaming of some magical rose garden over the horizon instead of enjoying the roses that are blooming outside our windows today *(Dale Carnegie)*.

- Most do not fully see this truth that life is difficult. Instead they moan more or less incessantly, noisily or subtly, about the enormity of their problems, their burdens, and their difficulties in life as if life were generally easy, as if life should be easy *(M. Scott Peck, The Road Less Travelled, 1978)*.

- The meaning of life is that it is to be *lived*, and it is not to be traded and conceptualized and squeezed into a pattern of systems *(Bruce Lee, Striking Thoughts, 2000, p. 3)*.

- There is no indignity in being afraid to die, but there is a terrible shame in being afraid to live *(Alydon – Doctor Who in "The Daleks")*.

- This is your life, and it's ending one minute at a time *(Narrator, Fight Club, 1999)*.

- My momma always said, "Life is like a box of chocolates. You never know what you're gonna get." *(Forrest Gump – Forrest Gump movie, 1994)*.

- The life that is unexamined is not worth living *(Plato/Apology 38)*

- You're not an owner in this life; you're just a steward *(Stephen King, Commencement Address, University of Maine, May 7, 2005)*.

- We see that both mind and body are expressions of life: they are parts of the whole of life. And we begin to understand their reciprocal relations in that whole. The life of man is the life of a moving being, and it would not be sufficient for him to develop body alone *(Alfred Adler, What Life Should Mean to You, 1931)*.

Wealth / Finances / Money / Material Possessions / Abundance

True Life Story by Surjit Kaur

"A penny saved is a penny earned."
-- George Herbert in *Outlandish Proverbs* (1633)

I have learned to be frugal over the years in order to manage family finances even on a low or limited income. My father would often quote this saying and I learned how it applied in life when I had my own family. What you earn is important but equally important is what you save. So when you spend money on anything, consider "what is its real value?" If you can manage expenses and learn to save, then you will in time grow in life. So that for a short-term pleasure you will never sacrifice your future. When you save even a penny, consider it a penny earned through discipline.
- Contributed by
 Surjit Kaur
 Retired Teacher & Personal Support Worker

Quotes on Wealth / Finances / Money / Material Possessions / Abundance

- Fame is but a fruit tree-
 so very unsound.
 It can never flourish
 'till its stock is in the ground *(Nick Drake, "Fruit Tree")*.

- No-one would remember the Good Samaritan if he'd only had good intentions; he had money as well *(Margaret Thatcher, TV Interview for London Weekend Television Weekend World, 6 January, 1980).*

- Pennies don't fall from heaven; they have to be earned here on earth *(Margaret Thatcher, Speech at Lord Mayor's Banquet, 12 November, 1979)*.

- Happiness lies not in the mere possession of money; it lies in the joy of e, in the thrill of creative effort *(Franklin D. Roosevelt, First Inaugural Address, 4 March 1933)*.

- I believe that thrift is essential to well-ordered living *(John D. Rockefeller)*.

- All the money in the world won't boost student achievement if parents make no effort to instil in their children the values of hard work and delayed gratification *(Barack Obama, The Audacity of Hope, 2006, p.63)*.

- I'd rather have a room full of cuddly teddy bears than a diamond necklace in a safe deposit locker *(Rani Mukherjee)*.

- They believe in the free market for profit but they want to socialize losses *(Bill Maher, Real Time with Bill Maher, 3 March 2008; regarding government assistance to banks)*.

- Conventional wisdom is to not put all your eggs in one basket. 80/20 wisdom is to choose a basket carefully, load all your eggs into it, and then watch it like a hawk *(Richard Koch)*.

- The market can stay irrational longer than you can stay solvent *(John Maynard Keynes)*.

- The importance of money flows from it being a link between the present and the future *(John Maynard Keynes)*.

- The day is not far off when the economic problem will take the back seat where it belongs, and the arena of the heart and the head will be occupied or reoccupied, by our real problems — the problems of life and of human relations, of creation and behaviour and religion *(John Maynard Keynes, First Annual Report of the Arts Council, 1945-1946).*

- When the accumulation of wealth is no longer of high social importance, there will be great changes in the code of morals *(John Maynard Keynes, "The Future", Essays in Persuasion, 1931, Ch. 5, JMK, CW, IX, pp.329 – 331).*

- I believe that thrift is essential to well-ordered living *(John D. Rockefeller).*

- I fully realize that no wealth or position can long endure, unless built upon truth and justice, therefore, I will engage in no transaction which does not benefit all whom it affects *(Napoleon Hill, Think and Grow Rich, 1938, p. 55).*

- No society can be flourishing and happy if the greater part of the members are poor and miserable *(Adam Smith, The Wealth of Nations, Chapter VIII).*

- But in all times men have been prone to believe that their happiness and well-being were to be secured by means of institutions rather than by their own conduct *(Samuel Smiles, Self Help, 1859).*

- Riches do not consist in the possession of treasures, but in the use made of them *(Napoléon Bonaparte).*

- Yes, I'm beautiful ... I am beautiful and famous — and yet the things I like about myself have nothing to do with that, because I don't use wealth and beauty to define myself *(Salma Hayek, Interview with Oprah Winfrey in O magazine, "Passion," September 2003).*

- Hunger is not quenched by fasting or even with obtaining loads of material possessions *(Guru Nanak).*

- A new model will have to emerge, and it cannot be based entirely on profit and consumerism *(Mikhail Gorbachev on the Global Financial Crisis," 05.11.2008)*.

- So this is the bottom line: cutthroat capitalism for the majority and "socialism," -- government help -- for those who are already rich. Yet, three or four years down the road, with the acute phase of the crisis behind us, these same people will be telling us that raw capitalism works best and that we should free them from regulation. Until the next, even more destructive crisis? *(Mikhail Gorbachev on the Global Financial Crisis," 05.11.2008)*.

- We can't leave people in abject poverty, so we need to raise the standard of living for 80% of the world's people, while bringing it down considerably for the 20% who are destroying our natural resources *(Jane Goodall)*.

- When I chased after money, I never had enough. When I got my life on purpose and focused on giving of myself and everything that arrived into my life, then I was prosperous *(Wayne Dyer)*.

- Increased means and increased leisure are the two civilizers of man *(Benjamin Disraeli, Speech to the Conservatives of Manchester, 1872-04-03)*.

- We need a more spiritual approach to success and to affluence which is the abundant flow of all good things to you *(Deepak Chopra)*.

- Surplus wealth is a sacred trust which its possessor is bound to administer in his lifetime for the good of the community *(Andrew Carnegie, The Best Fields for Philanthropy, from the North American Review, p. 684)*.

- The speed at which a business success is recognized, furthermore, is not that important as long as the company's intrinsic value is increasing at a satisfactory rate. In fact, delayed recognition can be an advantage: It may give us the chance to buy more of a good thing at a bargain price *(Warren Buffet).*

- If a business does well, the stock eventually follows *(Warren Buffet).*

- If you don't feel comfortable owning something for 10 years, then don't own it for 10 minutes *(Warren Buffet).*

- Risk comes from not knowing what you're doing *(Warren Buffet).*

- It's far better to buy a wonderful company at a fair price than a fair company at a wonderful price *(Warren Buffet).*

- Diversification is a protection against ignorance. It makes very little sense for those who know what they're doing *(Warren Buffet).*

- Most people get interested in stocks when everyone else is. The time to get interested is when no one else is. You can't buy what is popular and do well *(Warren Buffet).*

- Price is what you pay. Value is what you get *(Warren Buffet).*

- Material possessions in themselves are good. We would not survive for long without money, clothing, shelter and food. Yet if we refuse to share what we have with the hungry and the poor, we make of our possessions a false god. How many voices in our materialist society tell us that happiness is to be found by acquiring as many possessions and luxuries as we can! But this is to make possessions into a false god. Instead of bringing life, they bring death *(Pope Benedict XVI, World Youth Day 2008, held in Australia, Disadvantaged Youth, 18/07/08).*

- Thinking to get at once all the gold the goose could give, he killed it and opened it only to find – nothing *(Aesop, The Goose with the Golden Eggs).*

- Riches and honours acquired by unrighteousness are to me as a floating cloud *(Confucius)*.

- Do not store up for yourselves treasures on earth, where moth and rust destroy, and where thieves break in and steal. But store up for yourselves treasures in heaven, where moth and rust do not destroy, and where thieves do not break in and steal. For where your treasure is, there your heart will be also *(Matthew 6: 19-21)*.

- No one can serve two masters. Either you will hate the one and love the other, or you will be devoted to the one and despise the other. You cannot serve both God and Money *(Matthew 6:24)*.

- But seek first his kingdom and his righteousness, and all these things will be given to you as well *(Matthew 6: 33)*.

- People who want to get rich fall into temptation and a trap and into many foolish and harmful desires that plunge men into ruin and destruction. *(1 Timothy 6: 10)*.

- Whoever loves money never has money enough; whoever loves wealth is never satisfied with his income *(Ecclesiastes 5:10)*.

- Riches profit not in the day of wrath; but righteousness delivers from death *(Proverbs 11:4)*.

- A good man leaves an inheritance to his children's children *(Proverbs 13:22)*.

- An inheritance quickly gained at the beginning will not be blessed at the end *(Proverbs 20:21)*.

- The rich rule over the poor, and the borrower is slave to the lender *(Proverbs 22:7)*.

- Dishonest money dwindles away but money gathered little by little is increased *(Proverbs 13:11)*.

- Do not wear yourself out getting rich. Be smart enough to stop *(Proverbs 23:4)*.

- A good name is more desirable than great wealth. Respect is better than silver or gold *(Proverbs 22:1)*.

- Give to your family their due rights, as also to the poor, and to the wanderer: But squander not your wealth in the manner of the extravagant *(Quran 17:26)*.

- Anyone who is stingy is stingy only with his own soul. God is wealthy while you are poor *(Quran 47:38)*.

- One who becomes wealthy and takes pride in it: Not even a piece of straw can go along with you *(Guru Arjan Dev, Guru Granth Sahib, 278-10)*.

- Those who dwell upon the Lord's Name are the most wealthy and prosperous in the world *(Guru Arjan Dev, Guru Granth Sahib, 281-10)*.

- When the breath of life passes out of the mortal, tell me what becomes of his wealth? *(Saint Kabir, Guru Granth Sahib, 325-2)*.

- The Name of the Lord is the only permanent wealth; all other wealth comes and goes. Thieves cannot steal this wealth, nor can robbers take it away. This wealth of the Lord is embedded in the soul, and with the soul it shall depart *(Guru Amar Das, Guru Granth Sahib, 511:3-4)*.

- Wealthy are those who have a discerning intellect *(Guru Arjan Dev, Guru Granth Sahib, 1150:2)*.

- No one is a shareholder in this wealth of the Lord, and no one owns any of it. It has no boundaries or borders to be disputed *(Guru Ram Das, Guru Granth Sahib, 853:9)*.

- The Name is the wealth of my soul *(Guru Arjan Dev, 863:5)*.

- Subduing your pride, you shall receive the supreme wealth of God *(Guru Nanak Dev, Guru Granth Sahib, 904:14).*
- Money can buy you a house but can't buy you a home. Money can buy you food to put on your table but can't buy an appetite. Money can buy you one of the most finest Mattress in the world and a nice bed to sleep in but can't buy you sleep *(LeRoy Bailey Jr., From a sermon: We Need GOD).*

- There is no greater wealth than Virtue, And no greater loss than to forget it *(Thiruvalluvar, Tirukkural, Verse IV.2).*

- Money is like manure; it's not worth a thing unless it's spread around encouraging young things to grow *(Thornton Wilder, The Matchmaker, 1954).*

- The wealth required by nature is limited and is easy to procure; but the wealth required by vain ideals extends to infinity. *(Epicurus, Sovereign Maxims 15).*

- If we could put material things into their proper place, and use them without being attached to them, how much freer we would be. Then we wouldn't burden ourselves with things we don't need *(Peace Pilgrim, Peace Pilgrim: Her Life and Work in Her Own Words, 1992, p. 153).*

- All the perplexities, confusions, and distresses in America arise, not from defects in their constitution or confederation, not from a want of honour or virtue, so much as from downright ignorance of the nature of coin, credit, and circulation *(John Adams, Letter to Thomas Jefferson, 1787-08-25).*

Gratitude / Blessing / Gifts / Grace / Destiny

True Life Story Contribution
By Tony Kent

I have a number of favourite quotes and I have been impacted deeply by many of them, and I feel that the one that truly stands out as I write this is:

"The love you give is the love you get"
- from Sidi al Jamal Ar Rifai.

I would like to share a story with you about how this quote affected me so deeply and I believe actually changed the course of my life and also, I am hoping, the lives of my four children.

I had been going through an exceedingly painful separation and eventual divorce with Nathalie, the mother of my four children, and had spent a number of years in a really bad place emotionally, spiritually and also starting to run out of money. I was depressed, without ambition, and really wondering what had happened. I thought I had been a good father, good husband, and actually felt we had a really great marriage. I was wondering why and how bad things happen to good people and had even bought a book with that title.

For many years I had been a very successful fashion photographer, living in Paris and working for all the best magazines, travelling to amazing places, meeting beautiful and creative people, making lots of money and generally having a great time.

Then, my Mom got quite sick and I wanted to move back to the U.S.A. to be near her, and also I wanted my children to know more about the country I was born in. Nathalie was French, and both our kids at the time had been born in France. When we returned to the U.S.A. we had two more children, and we moved a number of times, from Dallas to California and eventually to
Santa Fe, New Mexico.

Nathalie had always had a big passion for the Southwest and especially anything that had something to do with cowboys or Indians. I was so busy living in my world, frequently travelling for my job, that I didn't consciously think that there was anything wrong at all with our relationship. I am not really sure that she did either. I really felt we were happy and that our life was really good. We lived on a large, almost 6 acre piece of land with a big house, over 6000 square feet, with horses, a beautiful table and 4 absolutely amazing children.

I later came to realize that my wife was not nearly as happy as I was. She had started to see other men and eventually met someone and fell in love. When she finally shared with me how unhappy she was, things had already advanced to a point where she wanted to leave and start a life on her own. I later came to understand a lot about what had happened, as well as the part I had played, where as for years I was mostly focused on playing the part of a victim.

During this time I got to a point that I was so depressed I actually was thinking up ways I could take my life, but in a way the children would think it was an accident. I was really in the dark night of the soul. I was desperate to find something to keep me going, to make me reach deep down inside to find something that would give me hope and help me to move to a better place.

Then one day I picked up the kids phone as it rang as I was walking by, and this was something I never did because it was not for me. For some reason this day I answered and that phone call led me to meet Kathleen and Derk Loeks who in turn introduced me to their spiritual teacher who lived in the Holy Land.

I eventually ended up going to Jerusalem and spending time with this man, who at the time was what is know as a "hidden teacher," and I have now spent almost 20 years immersed in his teachings. Upon returning to the states I started a non-profit to help disseminate these teachings and I don't think I have ever been happier than I am today.

Sidi's teachings are from the Sufi tradition, which is the mystical side of Islam and is about knowledge of God through the heart. You can learn more at www.healingthebrokenheart.org in a book I wrote about my meeting with him and what he taught me. There are also some videos of him teaching.

But, to return to my story; I was basically single parenting the four kids at that time, as they were all living with me because Nathalie was busy building her new life, and I had more or less stopped photography, and was working at home building a network marketing business. On day I came home from some errands and Justin and Tara, the two youngest kids, came running up to greet me; Tara jumping in my arms and Justin grabbing me around the legs. For the first time in almost 4 years I felt this cloud of depression lifting from me and I felt some actual joy in my heart. I was actually feeling happy for about 10 seconds.

Later that night after I had put the kids to sleep I was sitting in the living room thinking about those 10 seconds and wondering what had happened, and then it hit me. I remembered when I had gone to Jerusalem that Sidi had said *"the love you give is the love you get"* and so many of his teachings are about opening the heart and learning to love, and that love is the key to knowing God, and that knowing God is the key to our happiness.

And it was then that I realized that the reason I had been so unhappy is that I had stopped loving. I was waiting for the love to come to me, and I wanted that love from one person, and in one way, and I was so desperate that my heart had closed down. In 10 seconds my heart had opened up to the love I felt for my children, and I started to fully realize that if I wanted to be happy I was going to have to start loving again.

We find our joy by living as an extension of our creator, and he loves us all unconditionally, and so it is up to us to love unconditionally to experience a full connection with God.

I then started walking around the house and realizing how truly blessed I was. I had this amazing adobe home, full of beautiful things I had collected from all my travels, and everywhere I looked I found something to be grateful for. As I walked around through the different rooms I realized that I had stopped being thankful for all I had and was only focused on what I didn't have.

Giving gratitude is like giving love. The more love you give, the more the love grows inside you.

When love is pouring out of us, we usually feel pretty ecstatic, and for me, expressing gratitude feels pretty much the same. Giving gratitude is one of the best habits you can form and one of the best ways I know of opening yourself to be ready to accept true abundance.

Living from love and in gratitude is one of the most powerful healing methods, and when we are healed, we then can come from a place of wholeness and joy, and people will be attracted to us because joy and love are so charismatic.

I then went in the room where the kids were sleeping and sat down and watched them sleep. My heart was overflowing with love and my eyes were overflowing with tears, and as the love poured forth from deep within me, love that had been buried for so long, and I knew that night that I had been reborn and that my new life was really underway.

And I thought back to my time in Jerusalem where Sidi had looked into my heart and said *"the love you give is the love you get"* and it took me years to realize that he had given me the gift a long time before I ever really understood its value, or consciously knew what he was doing. I believe now he was planting a see in me.

I am just completing a new book and membership program call **Make Your Life Magical: Creating Wealth From Within** that is based on a lot of Sidi's teachings and how they have helped me use what he teaches to create a truly abundant existence. There are now hundreds of quotes from him I use all the time and I hope you will visit www.makeyourlifemagical.com and fill out the form there to be notified when the book and program are ready. You can download an e-book fro free there call *The Art of Abundance* which is a chapter from the new book.

Thanks for the opportunity to share and I look forward to further connections. Until then, live to love, love to serve, and make your life magical.

Many thanks and many blessings,

       Tony Kent
       San Anselmo, California,
       U.S.A.

       www.healingthebrokenheart.org
       www.makeyourlifemagical.com

QUOTES: GRATITUE/BLESSING/GIFTS/GRACE/ DESTINY

- When some 'blessings' come to you, do not drive them away through thanklessness *(Imam Ali)*.

- The blessing of the LORD, brings riches, and toil adds nothing to it *(Proverbs 10:22)*.

- Your greatness is measured by your gifts, not your possessions *(Harbhajan Singh Yogi)*.

- Blessedness is not the reward of virtue, but virtue itself *(Baruch Spinoza, Ethics, 1677, Part V: Of the Power of the Understanding, or of Human Freedom, Prop. 42)*.

- No one rejoices in blessedness, because he has controlled his lusts, but, contrariwise, his power of controlling his lusts arises from this blessedness itself *(Baruch Spinoza, Ethics, 1677, Part V: Of the Power of the Understanding, or of Human Freedom, Prop. 42, Proof)*.

- I'm becoming more and more myself with time. I guess that's what grace is. The refinement of your soul through time *(Jewel Kilcher, Interview with Chris Mundy, May 1997).*

- God's plan for each man transcends the limitation of the reasoning mind, and is always the square of life, containing health, wealth, love and perfect self-expression. Many a man is building for himself in imagination a bungalow when he should be building a palace *(Florence Scovell Shinn, The Game of Life and How to Play It, 1925).*

- I'm becoming more and more myself with time. I guess that's what grace is. The refinement of your soul through time *(Jewel Kilcher, Interview with Chris Mundy, May 1997).*

- Be grateful for what you do have, and you will find that it increases. I like to bless with love all that is in my life right now— my home, the heat, water, light, telephone, furniture, plumbing, appliances, clothing, transportation, jobs—the money I do have, friends, my ability to see and feel and taste and touch and walk and to enjoy this incredible planet *(Louise Hay, You Can Heal Your Life, 1984).*

- As I look back at the entire tapestry of my life I can see from the perspective of the present moment that every aspect of my life was necessary and perfect. Each step eventually led to a higher place, even though these steps often felt like obstacles or painful experiences *(Wayne Dyer, Real Magic: Creating Magic in Everyday Life, 1992).*

- Reflect upon your present blessings — of which every man has many — not on your past misfortunes, of which all men have some *(Charles Dickens, Sketches of Boz, 1836-1837, Characters, ch. 2).*

- A writer — and, I believe, generally all persons — must think that whatever happens to him or her is a resource. All things have been given to us for a purpose, and an artist must feel this more intensely. All that happens to us, including our humiliations, our misfortunes, our embarrassments, all is given to us as raw material, as clay, so that we may shape our art *(Twenty Conversations with Borges, Including a Selection of Poems: Interviews by Roberto Alifano, 1981–1983, 1984)*.

- Be generous in prosperity, and thankful in adversity *(Bahá'u'lláh)*.

- For everything created by God is good, and nothing is to be rejected if it is received with thanksgiving; for then it is consecrated by the word of God and prayer *(1 Timothy 4:3-5)*.

- A generous man is blessed because he shares his food with the poor *(Proverbs 22:9)*.
- Do not withhold your money, (for if you did so) Allah would withhold His blessings from you. *(Prophet Muhammad, Sahih Bukhair, Volume 2, Book 24, Number 513)*.

- Do not say about anything, "I am going to do that tomorrow," without adding, "If God wills *(Quran 18:23-24)*."

- This mind, body and wealth were given by God, who naturally adorns *us (Guru Arjan Dev, Guru Granth Sahib, 47-7)*.

- By Grace, you have land, gardens and wealth; keep God enshrined in your heart *(Guru Arjan Dev, Guru Granth Sahib, 270-7)*.

- The Supreme Lord gave the Order, and the rain automatically began to fall. Grain and wealth were produced in abundance as the earth was totally satisfied and satiated. Forever and ever, chant the Glorious Praises of the Lord, and pain and poverty will run away. People obtain that which they are pre-ordained to receive, according to the Divine Will *(Guru Arjan Dev, 321:17-19)*.

- As is wealth, so is adversity; whatever the Lord proposes, comes to pass *(Saint Kabir, Guru Granth Sahib, 337-13)*.

- You hold onto your body, mind and wealth as your own but you do not remember the Creator even for an instant *(Guru Arjan Dev, Guru Granth Sahib 805:14-15).*

- Righteous faith, wealth, sensual pleasure and salvation; the Lord bestows these four blessings *(Guru Arjan Dev, Guru Granth Sahib, 927:3).*

- One must always accept the unexpected *(The Doctor, Doctor Who in "The Leisure Hive").*

- I did not ask for the life I was given, but it was given nonetheless, and with it, I did my best *(Mr. Echo, Lost in The Cost of Living 3.5).*

- What we think about and thank about, we bring about *(Dr. John DeMartini, The Secret (film)).*

- Do not trouble your hearts overmuch with thought of the road tonight. Maybe the paths that you each shall tread are already laid before your feet, though you do not see them – Galadriel *(J.R.R. Tolkien, The Fellowship of the Ring, p. 388).*

- Things will go as they will; and there is no need to hurry to meet them – Treebeard *(J.R.R. Tolkien, The Two Towers, p. 609).*

- Accept whatever comes to you woven in the pattern of your destiny, for what could more aptly fit your needs? *(Marcus Aurelius).*

- Whatever happens at all happens as it should *(Marcus Aurelius, Meditations IV: 10).*

- In his heart a man plans his course, but the Lord determines his steps. *(Proverbs 16:9).*

- Gratitude is not only the greatest of virtues, but the parent of all others *(Cicero, Pro Plancio).*

- Whether we like it or not, we are all on a journey, a Quest if you will, every day of our lives, and the path we must take is full of perils, and our destiny can never be predicted in advance *(Alan Hirsch, The Leap of Faith, 2011, p. 20)*.

- This is the day which the Lord has made. Let us rejoice and be glad in it *(Psalm 118:24)*.

- Destiny is not a matter of chance, but of choice, not something to wish for, but to attain *(William Jennings Bryan as quoted in Wisdom for the Soul by Larry Chang, 2006, p. 122)*.

Health

- By health I mean the power to live a full, adult, living, breathing life in close contact with what I love — the earth and the wonders thereof — the sea — the sun *(Katherine Mansfield, Entry in her journal, 10 October 1922, published in The Journal of Katherine Mansfield (1927) ed. J. Middleton Murry)*.

- Natural forces within us are the true healers of disease *(Hippocrates, Aphorisms)*.

- The physician who teaches people to sustain their health is the superior physician. The physician who waits to treat people until after their health is lost is considered to be inferior *(Yellow Emperor's Classic on Internal Medicine, Chinese Medical Text from 500 BCE)*.

- The best doctors in the world are Doctor Diet, Doctor Quiet and Doctor Merryman *(Johnathan Swift, The Works of Jonathan Swift, 1843, p. 347)*.

- To lengthen thy life, lessen thy meals *(Benjamin Franklin, Poor Richard's Almanack, 2007, p. 45)*.

- What the placebo effect suggests is that we may be able to change what takes place in our bodies by changing our state of mind. Therefore, when we experience mind-altering processes – for example, meditation, hypnosis, visualization, psychotherapy, love and peace of mind – we open ourselves to the possibility of change and healing *(Bernie Siegel, Peace, Love & Healing, 1990, p. 19)*.

- I am convinced that unconditional love is the most powerful known stimulant of the immune system. If I told patients to raise their blood levels of immune globulins or killer T cells, no one would know how. But if I teach them to love themselves and others fully, the same changes happen automatically. The truth is, love heals *(Bernie Siegel, Love, Medicine & Miracles, 1990, p. 181)*.

Humour / Laughter

- Against the assault of laughter nothing can stand *(Mark Twain, The Mysterious Stranger, 1916)*.

- Laughter is America's most important export *(Walt Disney, The Quotable Walt Disney, 2001)*.

- It's not that I'm afraid to die, I just don't want to be there when it happens *(Woody Allen, Without Feathers, 1975)*.

- If only God would give me some clear sign! Like making a large deposit in my name in a Swiss bank *(Woody Allen, Without Feathers, 1975)*.

- The key is, to not think of death as an end, but as more of a very effective way to cut down on your expenses *(Woody Allen, Love and Death, 1975)*.

- The important thing, I think, is not to be bitter... if it turns about that there is a God, I don't think that he is evil. I think that the worst thing you could say is that he is, basically, an under-achiever *(Woody Allen, Love and Death, 1975)*.

- A person without a sense of humour is like a wagon without springs – jolted by every pebble in the road *(Henry Ward Beecher as quoted in Living Simply by Sara Orem, Larry Demarest, 1994, p. 67).*

- Against the assault of laughter nothing can stand. You are always fussing and fighting with your other weapons. Do you ever use that one? *(Mark Twain, The Complete Short Stories of Mark Twain, 2008, p. 481).*

- Laughter is the shortest distance between two people *(Victor Borge as quoted in Quote Unquote by M.P. Singh, 2005, p. 187).*

Manifestation / Abundance

- Your soul, breath of life, mind and body shall blossom forth in lush profusion; this is the true purpose of life *(Guru Arjan Dev, 47-19).*

- You are built not to shrink down to less but to blossom into more *(Oprah Winfrey, O Magazine, February 2003).*

- The lack of money is the root of all evil *(Mark Twain, Merle Johnson, More Maxims of Mark, 1927).*

- In the end, you're measured not by how much you undertake but by what you finally accomplish *(Donald Trump, Trump: the Art of the Deal, 1987).*

- God's plan for each man transcends the limitation of the reasoning mind, and is always the square of life, containing health, wealth, love and perfect self-expression. Many a man is building for himself in imagination a bungalow when he should be building a palace *(Florence Scovell Shinn, The Game of Life and How to Play It, 1925).*

Patience

- If someone may see something then they may ask for it or someone may give it. But no one can take a share of this wealth of the Lord by force *(Guru Amar Das, Rag Bilawal, 853-7)*.

- Slow and steady wins the race *(Aesop, The Hare and the Tortoise)*.

- There are two main human sins from which all the others derive: impatience and indolence.... Yet perhaps there is only one major sin: impatience *(Franz Kafka, The Blue Octavo Notebooks, 1954: Analogy of allowing vegetables to cook slowly and properly)*.

- If you are wholly perplexed and in straits, have patience, for patience is the key to joy *(Rumi, Rumi Daylight: A Daybook of Spiritual Guidance, 1990 trans. by Camille Adams Helminsk and Kabir Helminski)*.

- Time, that aged nurse, Rocked me to patience *(John Keats, Endymion, 1818, Bk. I, l. 705)*.

- That I did not fail was due in part to patience *(Jane Goodall)*.

- No-thing great is created suddenly, any more than a bunch of grapes or a fig. If you tell me that you desire a fig, I answer you that there must be time. Let it first blossom, then bear fruit, then ripen *(Epictetus, Discourses, Book I, ch. 15)*.

Simplicity

- Though I am grateful for the blessings of wealth, it hasn't changed who I am. My feet are still on the ground. I'm just wearing better shoes *(Oprah Winfrey, O Magazine)*.

- That man is richest whose pleasures are the cheapest *(Henry David Thoreau, Journals, March 11, 1856)*.

- Care of the soul is a continuous process that concerns itself not so much with 'fixing' a central flaw as with attending to the small details of everyday life, as well as to major decisions and *changes (Thomas Moore, Care of the Soul: A Guide for Cultivating Depth and Sacredness in Everyday Life, 1992).*

- Soul cannot thrive in a fast-paced life because being affected, taking things in and chewing on them, requires time *(Thomas Moore, Care of the Soul: A Guide for Cultivating Depth and Sacredness in Everyday Life, 1992).*

- If you cannot do great things, do small things in a great way *(Napoleon Hill, The Law of Success, 1937).*

- That man is richest whose pleasures are the cheapest *(Henry David Thoreau, Journals, March 11, 1856).*

- Luxurious food and drinks, in no way protect you from harm. Wealth beyond what is natural, is no more use than an overflowing container. Real value is not generated by theaters, and baths, perfumes or ointments, but by philosophy *(Epicurus, Written by Diogenes of Oenoanda).*

- Style, harmony, grace and good rhythm depend on simplicity *(Plato, Republic III: 400-D).*

- Even with only coarse rice to eat, water to drink and my bended arm for a pillow, I can still have joy *(Confucius Analects 7:15).*

- Man's greatest wealth is to live on a little with contented mind; for a little is never lacking *(Lucretius, De Rerum Natura V: 1117).*

- The greatest wealth is to live content with little *(Plato, The Republic).*

- If a man does not keep pace with his companions, perhaps it is because he hears a different drummer. Let him step to the music which he hears, however measured or far away *(Henry David Thoreau, Walden, 1854).*

- Voluntary simplicity is an attitude, not a budget: thoughtful consumption, resistance to artificially created "needs," sensitivity to the limits of natural resources, a more human scale for living and working ... Voluntary simplicity is neither altruistic nor a sacrifice. It can even be hedonistic. Simple lifestyles can become a pleasure in themselves *(Marilyn Ferguson, The Aquarian Conspiracy, 1980).*

- The simplified life is a sanctified life, much more calm, much less strife *(Peace Pilgrim, Peace Pilgrim: Her Life and Work in Her Own* Words, *1982).*

- Not buying something, not going somewhere, and not watching something can each be an effective application of the simplicity rule. Living closer to nature helps simplify because nature, though complex, keeps us in tune with basic rhythms and pleasures that never change and that provide grounding *(Thomas Moore, Original Self, 2000).*

Social Justice / Social Issues " "

- No society can be flourishing and happy if the greater part of the members are poor and miserable *(Adam Smith, The Wealth of Nations, Chapter VIII).*

- I have hope because the positive aspects of globalization are enabling nations and peoples to become politically, economically and socially interdependent, making war an increasingly unacceptable option *(Mohamed ElBaradei, Nobel Lecture, 2005).*

- Imagine what would happen if the nations of the world spent as much on development as on building the machines of war. Imagine a world where every human being would live in freedom and dignity. Imagine a world in which we would shed the same tears when a child dies in Darfur or Vancouver. Imagine a world where we would settle our differences through diplomacy and dialogue and not through bombs or bullets. Imagine if the only nuclear weapons remaining were the relics in our museums. Imagine the legacy we could leave to our children. Imagine that such a world is within our grasp *(Mohamed ElBaradei, Nobel Lecture, 2005).*

- It is better and more satisfactory to acquit a thousand guilty persons than to put a single innocent one to death *(Maimonides, Sefer Hamitzvot, translated by Charles B. Chavel, 1967).*

- The system concedes nothing without demand *(Steve Biko, I Write What I Like, 1978).*

- The most potent weapon in the hands of the oppressor is the mind of the oppressed *(Steve Biko, I Write What I Like, 1978).*

- If you are neutral in situations of injustice, you have chosen the side of the oppressor. If an elephant has its foot on the tail of a mouse and you say that you are neutral, the mouse will not appreciate your neutrality *(Desmond Tutu, quoted in Ending Poverty As We Know It by William P. Quigley, p. 8).*

- Freedom and liberty lose out by default because good people are not *vigilant (Desmond Tutu quoted in Lives That Make a Difference by P.J. Clarke, 2011, p. 270).*

- There are different kinds of justice. Retributive justice is largely Western. The African understanding is far more restorative - not so much to punish as to redress or restore a balance that has been knocked askew *(Desmond Tutu quoted in Understanding African Philosophy by Richard H. Bell, 2002, p.90).*

- If real development is to take place, the people have to be involved *(Julius Nyerere, Uhuru na Maendeleo, 1973).*

- We spoke and acted as if, given the opportunity for self-government, we would quickly create utopias. Instead injustice, even tyranny, is rampant *(Julius Nyerere quoted in The Africans by David Lamb, 1985).*

- The real tragedy of our postcolonial world is not that the majority of people had no say in whether or not they wanted this new world; rather, it is that the majority have not been given the tools to negotiate this new world *(Chimamanda Ngozi Adichie, Half of a Yellow Sun, 2007, p. 129).*

- In order for us human beings to commit ourselves personally to the inhumanity of war, we find it necessary to first dehumanize our opponents, which is itself a violation of the beliefs of all religions. Once we characterize our adversaries as beyond the scope of God's mercy and grace, their lives lose all value *(Jimmy Carter, Nobel Lecture, Oslo, December 10, 2002).*

- Be the change you wish to see in the world *(Mahatma Gandhi).*

- If a free society cannot help the many who are poor, it cannot save the few who are rich *(John F. Kennedy, Inaugural Address, January 20, 1961).*

- And he lifted up his eyes on his disciples, and said, Blessed be you poor: for yours is the kingdom of God *(Luke 6:20).*

- It is easier for a camel to go through the eye of a needle, than for a rich man to enter into the kingdom of God *(Mark 10:25, Matthew 19:24).*

- We must rapidly begin the shift from a "thing-oriented" society to a "person-oriented" society. When machines and computers, profit motives and property rights are considered more important than people, the giant triplets of racism, materialism, and militarism are incapable of being conquered *(Martin Luther King, Jr., Beyond Vietnam, 1967).*

Success/Accomplishment/Achievement/Excellence

True Life Story by Surjit Kaur

"**Excellence is doing ordinary things extraordinarily well.**"-- John W. Gardner

I believe that this quote expresses the idea that greatness lies in bringing the extraordinary into your everyday life even in daily tasks we consider boring. When you do these ordinary tasks with an extraordinary attitude the task is transformed and elevated to your responsibility, your calling and to your relationships. As a single mother of three children, I decided a long time ago to always do everything with love of my family, whether it is working at a normal job, cooking, laundry, cleaning or taking care of seniors, I always performed my work with love for people in my life. Through that love and sincere effort, I found that my work offered me comfort, strength and gave me hope that I can better my own life and that of my children.

- Contributed by **Surjit Kaur**
  Retired Teacher & Personal Support Worker

True Life Story by Robert-Anthony Browne

INTRODUCTION TO INSPIRATIONAL SAYINGS

Over the years I have assembled my own inspirational maxims based on my experiences aligned with the vicissitudes of my life's journey. L There may be similar well known sayings, but as far as I am aware these maxims are original in their exact wording and personal to me.

Adages and sayings are very important for all of us who, from time to time, need inspiration during "valley" periods. When an inspirational quote is referenced our spirits are buoyed and it is not long before we have assimilated the particular event into our repertoire of our life's experiences and become more mature.

THE POTENTIAL FOR GREATNESS IS WITHIN EVERY PERSON

What is "greatness?" "Greatness," in my opinion, is subjective and individualistic. The metaphor "One person's ceiling is another person's floor" reminds us that we should set our own standards of achievement and accomplishment not influenced by other peoples' goals and success. People should establish their own paradigms of excellence and be the best that they can be according to what motivates them to excel.

This maxim reminds me that as human beings we can all maximize our potential to our own individual standards and push ourselves to limits that we might not have thought possible until we try. Famous people, who have sometimes overcome tremendous odds, are our inspiration to believe that we, too, can raise our own standards of excellence and be all that we have the potential to be, given our own individual circumstances. A forerunner, or role model, is an excellent guideline for us to emulate.

Many people do not embark on their success journey because of fear, eternal fine tuning of their project, procrastination or vacillation. A thought to ponder: "Why does the thrill of soaring have to begin with the fear of falling?"

OUR SUCCESS IN REACHING OUR OBJECTIVE IS LIMITED ONLY BY OUR OWN SPHERE OF THOUGHT

Apparently human beings, on average, use only three percent of their brain's capacity. I like the idea of what has been termed "possibility thinking," whereby people can draw on inspiration which will elevate their thinking to new heights and awareness of their potential. The saying that "it's all in the mind" is so true. People can experience such a rush of endorphin release when they make a new discovery, when that "eureka" moment happens and they realize that they have reached a new level of understanding and therefore an expanded mindset.
May this maxim encourage us all to not be mentally lazy but to keep on stretching our mind's capacity for growth and understanding.

SUCCESS IS VERY SIMPLE: PEOPLE COMPLICATE IT

People seem to complicate success principles, being their own worst enemies, thinking that because many people live in mediocrity that those who have "made it" have superior talent or have experienced lucky breaks or the like. People often feel that they have to be super human to achieve their ultimate dream(s) until they reach enlightened awareness and have a "eureka" breakthrough; at which point they wonder why on earth things had seemed so complicated previously. If we associate with people who are successful by our standards (whom we might not normally associate with) and that we would like to emulate then we realize that we, too, have what it takes and wonder why in the world we have made it seem so complicated.
It has been said that if we could shadow the heroes of our chosen field intensively during their typical day for a period of three days that we would be totally changed and would operate thenceforth in the realm of the stratosphere of our dreams (which, incidentally, are no longer "dreams" but the norm)
The key is to find our unique talents and then to see how we can make the most of them. If we find where our skills lie, not being

influenced by people who have become successful in endeavours that are right for them but foreign to our talents, then success will become a lot simpler. I believe that when we have discovered our niche circumstances have a way of falling into place more naturally and we are often more prolific with our accomplishments because we are naturally gifted in that particular field. We must recognize what we enjoy and excel at.

TODAY'S *VALLEY* IS THE *MOUNTAIN PEAK* OF TOMORROW

Without the "lows" we would not appreciate the "highs." The "lows" are really where our growth takes place for future accomplishment. It is through these *seemingly* down times that we grow from our increased knowledge gained from the experience. When we have survived the ordeal we realize that we are now soaring towards the mountain peak of our dreams because of that seemingly adverse situation which, in reality, has been a *blessing in disguise.* The chapters of our life's storybook are fascinating and some of our fondest memories, in retrospect, are when we have survived and been victorious over those lows, which are really synonymous with growth.

If we become embittered by seemingly hostile situations then we have lost the meaning of the lesson which is meant to mature us. We must extricate our lives from bitterness as quickly as possible, often with the help of a counsellor/coach, so as to absorb the experience and the lesson gained there from, so as to progress our lives forwards.

PEOPLE ARE LIMITED ONLY BY THEIR SPHERE OF THOUGHT

Apparently human beings, on average, use only *three percent* of their brain's capacity. How much more of our *potential* we have to tap into! I like the idea of what has been termed *"possibility thinking,"* whereby people can draw on inspiration which will elevate their thinking to new heights and awareness of their potential. The saying that *"it's all in the mind"* is so true. People can experience such a rush of *endorphin release* .when they make a new discovery, when that *"aha!"* moment occurs and they realize that they have reached a *new level* of understanding and therefore and *expanded mindset*.

May this maxim encourage us all to not be mentally lazy but to keep on *stretching our mind* for growth and understanding.

CONSTRUCTIVE THOUGHTS AND CONVERSATIONS

"**Great** minds discuss IDEAS,
Average minds discuss events,
Small minds discuss people ...."

- Eleanor Roosevelt

When people have goals and objectives they are receptive to new ideas and brainstorming. When this type of conversation occurs, with a like minded person(s), it is enormously enriching and participants mostly feel that there has been a breakthrough in whatever area the person wants to improve upon.

A great mind will create its own successful event and not be content to just talk in wonderment about somebody else's success, which may be used as a *guideline* for the success of its own event.

May each of us have goals and objectives that are nourished by great *ideas*.

BEING OBSERVANT OF THE BENEFITS OF EVERY SEEMINGLY ADVERSE SITUATION

"Every cloud has a silver lining"
- John Milton

When we are progressive people we must look for the benefit of every *seemingly* adverse situation. We can often learn more from these types of situations, from a personal growth perspective, than if things were always going smoothly. I do not mean to give the impression that we should invite adverse circumstances into our lives, but we should be observant of any lesson(s) associated with the experience that could make us bigger and better people.

- Contributed by **Robert-Anthony Browne,** Oakville, Ontario Progressive Counsellor/Performance Success Coach (business/personal)/ Real Estate Investment Coach (groups/individuals) Contact Information: 289-681-1265 Synergism_2@msn.com

Robert-Anthony Browne featured in the chapter "Miracles In Business" ("Robert Brown") of the best selling book "Miracles" by Geoff and Hope Price.

Quotes: Success/Accomplishment/Achievement/ Excellence

- I think your job is just to be there 100% - you work hard and there are no shortcuts to success *(Preity Zinta).*

- Success usually comes to those who are too busy looking for it *(Henry David Thoreau).*

- There's no abiding success without commitment *(Anthony Robbins).*

- Success makes so many people hate you. I wish it wasn't that way. It would be wonderful to enjoy success without seeing envy in the eyes of those around you *(Marilyn Monroe, The Films of Barbra Streisand, 2001 by Christopher Nickens and Karen Swenson).*

- You've got to be a success; nobody has patience with failures *(Amitabh Bachchan, Filmfare Interview, 1 December 1972, published in Filmfare February 2005 issue).*

- Success has nothing to do with happiness *(Gillian Anderson).*

- Success is 99% failure *(Soichiro Honda).*

Success can only be achieved through repeated failure and introspection *(Soichiro Honda, Davis, W., 1991 "The Innovators", in Henry, J. and Walker, D. Managing Innovation, London, Sage).*

- The real problem is not to get to the top but to stay there *(Amitabh Bachchan, Filmfare Interview, 1 December 1972, published in Filmfare February 2005 issue).*

- I would sooner fail than not be among the greatest *(John Keats, Letter to James Hessey, October 9, 1818).*

- For success, like happiness, cannot be pursued; it must ensue, and it only does so as the unintended side-effect of one's personal dedication to a cause greater than oneself or as the by-product of one's surrender to a person other than oneself. Happiness must happen, and the same holds for success: you have to let it happen by not caring about it *(Viktor Frankl, Man's Search For Meaning, 60th anniversary edition, p. 16-17).*

- Many of life's failures are people who did not realize how close they were to success when they gave up *(Thomas Edison).*

- You are successful and creative only when you see an opportunity in every difficulty *(Chinmayananda).*

- Success or achievement is not the final goal. It is the 'spirit' in which you act that puts the seal of beauty upon your life *(Chinmayananda).*

- Develop success from failures. Discouragement and failure are two of the surest stepping stones to success *(Dale Carnegie).*

- Success often lies just the other side of *failure (Leo Buscaglia).*

- The winners in this life know the rules of the game and have a plan, so that their efficiency is comparatively exponential to that of people who don't. No big mystery, just fact *(Phil McGraw, Life Strategies: Doing What Works, Doing What Matters, 1999).*

- The heights by great men reached and kept
  Were not attained by sudden flight,
  But they, while their companions slept,
  Were toiling upward in the night *(Henry Wadsworth Longfellow, The Ladder of St. Augustine, 1858).*

- *Don't fear failure.* — Not failure, but low aim, is the crime. In great attempts it is glorious even to fail *(Striking Thoughts, 2000, p. 121).*

- Be not ashamed of mistakes and thus make them crimes *(Confucius).*

- There is plenty of room at the top because very few people care to travel beyond the average route. And so most of us seem satisfied to remain within the confines of mediocrity *(Nnamdi Azikiwe, My Odyssey, 1971).*

- You will begin to succeed with your life when the pains and problems of others matter to you *(T.B. Joshua, The News Magazine - Nigeria, December 17, 2007).*

- We are what we repeatedly do. Excellence then, is not an act, but a habit *(Aristotle).*

- People with a high level of personal mastery live in a continual learning mode. They never "arrive" *(Peter Senge, The Fifth Discipline: The Art and Practice of The Learning Organization, 1990).*

- Success is the result of preparation, hard work, learning from failure, loyalty to those for whom you work, and persistence *(Colin Powell as quoted in Wisdom for the Soul by Larry Chang, 2006, p. 684).*

Sustainability

- Our personal consumer choices have ecological, social, and spiritual consequences. It is time to re-examine some of our deeply held notions that underlie our lifestyles *(David Suzuki)*.

- Every passing generation is but a mere trustee of this grand inheritance of nature. As trustees we are duty-bound to pass this inheritance on to future generations. Preserving the memory of what we have received is an important way in which we can ensure that it survives the ravages of time *(Manmohan Singh, Kaziranga is a Global Treasure, New Delhi, 8 April 2005)*.

- We must protect the forests for our children, grandchildren and children yet to be born. We must protect the forests for those who can't speak for themselves such as the birds, animals, fish and trees *(Qwatsinas)*.

-

Action / Ability / Work / Duty / Career / Vocation

True Life Story on Action by Raj Kamal
Karm kar phal ki chinta mat kar (Bhagvad Gita)

Translated into English this means: "Do your actions or duties and do not worry about the results i.e. the fruits."

If you start thinking of the fruits then you end up focusing too much on future gain.

This quote reminds you to focus on just doing your action or duty to your best ability and with a deep sense of joy and responsibility. The future will take care of itself and we can leave anxiety and worry aside. To do this means that you need to trust in the Universe.

I live this in my life as it comes so I find it easier to go with the flow. I take actions with ease instead of being stressed and over thinking possibilities.

This relaxed state of mind allows for better decision-making and response to any opportunity or challenge before you.

I believe these kinds of quotes have been created in holy books to give their followers a healthy and relaxed life.

Usually people keep on worrying about their future and as a result this can increase hypertension, anxiety, depression, heart disease and other stress-related problems.
- Contributed by **Raj Kamal** Ontario, Canada

True Life Story by Shelley Kay Manos

I find inspiration in my own life! Here's my life in a nutshell:

I am 54 years old and am excited about moving to Orchid Bay Belize, in April of this year with my husband Rocky Manos, my father, my brother, and only 31 year old son, Jason.

I was born and raised in Portland, Oregon and I lived in Kalispell, Montana on a 250 acre farm, for almost seven years. Then I moved back to Portland after my mother passed away in February 2012. I reconnected with my seventh grade sweetheart in August 2010, at our 35th Gresham, Oregon High School Reunion. Our love rekindled and Rocky and I just married on September 15th, 2012. My favourite saying is the following:

"Do what you love. If you don't know what brings you joy, ask...What is my joy?" Rhonda Byrne

I try to live by this quote. As you commit to your joy, you will attract an avalanche of joyful things in your life because you are radiating joy! I've always felt blessed in my own life by this principle."

- Contributed by **Shelley Kay Manos**

(Moving to Orchid Bay, Belize)
lioness_skk@yahoo.com
Rock & Shell Travel Services
www.RockyManos.com

Quotes: Action/ Ability/ Work/ Duty/Career / Vocation

- Inspiration exists, but it has to find you working - *La inspiración existe, pero tiene que encontrarte trabajando (Pablo Picasso).*

- The world owes no man a living but that it owes every man an opportunity to make a living *(John D. Rockefeller).*

- I know of nothing more despicable and pathetic than a man who devotes all the hours of the waking day to the making of money for money's sake *(John D. Rockefeller).*

- Work is the rent you pay for the room you occupy on earth *(Queen Elizabeth II).*

- Inspiration exists, but it has to find you working - *La inspiración existe, pero tiene que encontrarte trabajando (Pablo Picasso).*

- Big pay and little responsibility are circumstances seldom found together *(Napoleon Hill, The Law of Success, 1937, p. 109).*

- If you really want something, and really work hard, and take advantage of opportunities, and never give up, you will find a way *(Jane Goodall).*

Take the initiative. Go to work, and above all co-operate and don't hold back on one another or try to gain at the expense of another *(Buckminster Fuller, Operating Manual for Spaceship Earth, 1963).*

- If you will not fight your battle of life because in selfishness you are afraid of the battle, then your resolution is in vain: Nature will compel you *(Bhagavad Gita).*

- But one who, with strong body and serving mind, gives up his power to worthy work. Not seeking gain Arjuna! Such a one is honourable. Do your allotted task! *(Bhagavad Gita)*

- The big secret in life is that there is no big secret. Whatever your goal, you can get there if you're willing to work *(Oprah Winfrey, O Magazine)*.

- Action is the foundational key to all success *(Anthony Robbins)*.

- Balance your thoughts with action. — If you spend too much time thinking about a thing, you'll never get it done *(Bruce Lee, Striking Thoughts, 2000, p. 43)*.

- God doesn't require us to succeed; he only requires that you try *(Mother Theresa)*.

- To action alone have you a right and never at all to its fruits *(Bhagavad Gita 2:47)*.

- The superior person is modest in speech, but exceeds in actions *(Confucius)*.

- So in everything, do to others what you would have them do to you, for this sums up the Law and the Prophets *(Golden Rule from Matthew 7:12)*.

- All hard work brings a profit, but mere talk leads only to poverty *(Proverbs 14:23)*.

- I have seen everything that is done under the sun; and behold, all is vanity and a striving after wind *(Ecclesiastes 1:2-3)*.

- Like the waves in great rivers, there is no turning back of that which has previously been done *(Maitri Upanishad 4.2)*.

- Creating, yet not possessing. Working, yet not taking credit. Work is done, and then forgotten. Therefore it lasts forever *(Lao Tzu, Tao Te Ching 2)*.

- Through selfless action, the sage attains fulfillment *(Lao Tzu, Tao Te Ching 7)*.

- Retire when the work is done. This is the way of heaven *(Lao Tzu, Tao Te Ching 9)*.

- A rash action is worse than no action at all *(The Doctor, Doctor Who in "The Edge of Destruction")*.

- Well done is that action of doing which one repents not later, and the fruit of which one reaps with delight and happiness *(The Buddha, Dhammapada 68)*.

- One who plants thorns must never expect to gather roses *(Panchatantra, "The Ignorant Physician," Fable viii)*.

- For the things we have to learn before we can do them, we learn by doing them *(Aristotle, Nicomachean Ethics, II, I, 1103a)*.

- The world cares very little about what a man or woman knows; it is what a man or woman is able to do that counts *(Booker T. Washington)*.

- We all have ability. The difference is how we use it *(Stevie Wonder)*.

- Remember this— that there is a proper dignity and proportion to be observed in the performance of every act of life *(Marcus Aurelius, Meditations IV: 32)*.

- Have I done something for the general interest? Well then I have had my reward. Let this always be present to thy mind, and never stop doing such good *(Marcus Aurelius, Meditations XI: 4)*.

- Let your soul fear Allah and consider what deeds you have put forth for tomorrow. For God is aware of what you do *(Quran 59:18)*.

- Everyone has been made for some particular work, and the desire for that work has been put in every heart *(Rumi quoted in Marry Your Muse by Jan Phillips, 1997, p. 75)*.

- Let the beauty of what you love be what you do *(Rumi quoted in The Law of Attraction: Making It Work for You by Deborah Morrison and Arvind Singh, 2009, p. 58)*.

- The way of the sage is to act but not to compete *(Lao Tsu, Tao te Jing)*.

- There is nothing better than for you to rejoice in every deed in harmony with the moment. For doing is your purpose; in doing is your meaning. Leave the result to those who come after you. And attend solely to doing well that which must be done at all *(Ecclesiastes 3:21-22)*.

- That knowledge which remains only on your tongue is very superficial. The intrinsic value of knowledge is that you act upon it *(Hazrat Ali)*.

- Well done is better than well said *(Benjamin Franklin)*.

- The purpose must result in strivings; intent has to be translated into action *(Mihaly Csikszentmihalyi, Flow: The Psychology of Optimal Experience, 1990)*.

- Until knowledge, awareness, insights and understandings are translated into action, they are of no value *(Phil McGraw, Life Strategies: Doing What Works, Doing What Matters, 1999)*.

- Without action upon an idea, there will be no manifestation, no results, and no reward *(Miguel Ruiz, The Four Agreements, 1997)*.

- You miss 100 per cent of the shots you never take (*Wayne Gretzky*).

- Don't skate to where the puck is – skate to where it's going to be (*Wayne Gretzky*)

- Remember upon the conduct of each depends the fate of all (*Alexander the Great*).

Ordinary Everyday Mystic

Change is a constant, ordinary
in Nature, slow and steady,
obscured by our mind's absorption
until a critical mass *aha* moment.

Walking outside to the mailbox
greeted by fall's embrace
coloured leaves falling and swirling,
gracefully decorating the ground.

And my special love, the wind
swaying the trees by its force
creating the soothing swishing sound
racing by my ears as I breath it in.

Never boring sights and sounds—
objectively it's *predictable fall weather,*
yet my subjective experience is exhilarated,
joyfully touched amidst aesthetic beauty.

Though fall weather is *expected*
nothing is remotely ordinary with
many shades and nuances of colours,
flowers bloom before the frost.

Behind the dancing, singing trees
incredible blue sky painted
by moving, multi-coloured clouds—
if this is ordinary, no words for extraordinary!

Yet a peaceful, satisfied mind is required
to observe and really appreciate this
by happily living with spiritual practice
instead of being mad for external happiness.

Transforming "ordinary" life into super-extraordinary
bringing the artistic beauty Spirit Source
into our lives—not just intellectually
but by our honest attempt to give our heart and soul.

Until we are a realized lover of Divinity
our endeavour is to bring Spirit into every moment
seeing Spirit in the smallest and greatest
in wind, rain, drought, seasons, food, birth and death.
Let us arise from our dream without
identifying our soul with fleeting matter
or struggling for existence to avoid death
thinking the Universe empty without purpose.

Firmly embracing Divine Love we find
everything is favourable for service,
the world becomes the abode of joy
even sorrow or calamity are God's embrace!

Supreme Love become our magnificent obsession
as life revolves around our heart's aspiration,
pleasure and satisfaction in spiritual practice
turns us into a mystic, just living our everyday life.

Karnamrita Das has been a practitioner of Bhakti or Devotional Yoga for 42 years. He lives with his near Hanging Rock Park, North Carolina, idyllic countryside for spiritual cultivation. He has a blog on Krishna.com, http://www.krishna.com/blogs/karnamritadas from which his new book, *Give to Live*, has just been released, and is available at Amazon.com. Email: karnamrita@yahoo.com.

"I've found constancy and balance between creativity and normality."
- Julian Lennon

"Sometimes our emotions make it hard
For us to see that
At the heart of loving is respect and honesty"
- Lyric excerpt from song *Take Me Home,*
Songwriters, Ezrin, Robert A / Clayton, Justin / Lennon, Julian

"If we believed in love
We wouldn't worry 'bout the problems of tomorrow,
There'd be a strength inside of us
To last the rest of our lives"
- Lyric excerpt from song *Believe,*
Songwriter, Julian Lennon

Closing thought – in reading and reflecting on the words of wisdom throughout this book, the reader experiences profound thoughts, which can lead to the further, deeper experiences of processing, personalizing and reflecting upon the insightful knowledge within and incorporating all of this into one's own world view and one's own life experience.

"The only source of knowledge is experience"
Albert Einstein

About the Authors:

Deborah Morrison is an Author, Transformational Coach, and Speaker from Hamilton, Ontario, Canada, who is inspired by the healing power of the written word, nature, and people. She has written extensively on natural therapies, yoga, psychology, and metaphysics and has attained Yoga Teacher's Training Certification after studying with world-renowned Yoga and Meditation Master, and Great Soul, *Swami Vishnudevananda*.

Deborah holds an Honours B.A. Social Sciences in Religious Studies/Sociology from McMaster University and a Master's Certification in Counselling Science. She is the former Vice President of the *Tower Poetry Society*, the first and foremost ongoing poetry society in North America. Deborah is the author of *Mystical Poetry*, and *In The Garden: Where Inspiration Grows*, and is co-author, with Arvind Singh, of *Nexus; The Law of Attraction: Making it Work For You;* and *Wise Words: Insightful Reflections*.

Arvind Singh is co-author with Deborah Morrison of bestsellers *The Law of Attraction – Making it Work for You!* and *Nexus*. He is an inspirational writer, spiritual seeker and librarian with a Masters degree in Library and Information Sciences. He is philosophical, spiritual and eclectic, with an interest in a variety of topics including: personal growth, self-development, mysticism, environment, quantum physics, travel and cultural studies.

With an interest in different cultures while growing up in multicultural Canada, Arvind has found many sources of wisdom from a variety of traditions. His own background, as a practicing Sikh, shows his commitment to faith. He has also been involved in Interfaith dialogue to explore what makes us the same even with our apparent differences. He has written several articles in both English and South Asian languages, and has discussed his articles and books in media interviews. He enjoys taking the reader on a journey through words with spiritual depth, understanding and inspiration.

Wise Words

Manor House
905-648-2193
www.manor-house.biz